SUCCESS AFTER 40

LATE BLOOMERS WHO MADE IT BIG

Allan Zullo with Bill Hartigan

Andrews and McMeel
A Universal Press Syndicate Company
Kansas City

Library of Congress Cataloging-in-Publication Data

Zullo, Allan.
        Success after 40 : late bloomers who made it big / Allan Zullo with
    Bill Hartigan.
            p.   cm.
        ISBN 0-8362-2190-7 (pb.)
    . 1. Celebrities—United States—Biography. 2. Middle aged persons—
    United States—Biography. 3. Success—Case studies. 4. United States—
    Biography. 5. Biography—20th century. I. Hartigan, Bill. II. Title.
        CT215.Z85   1996
        920.073—dc20   96-24873
                                                                        CIP

Design and composition by Steve Brooker at *Just Your Type*

ATTENTION: SCHOOLS AND BUSINESSES
Andrews and McMeel books are available at quantity discounts with bulk purchase for educational, business, or sales promotional use. For information, please write to: Special Sales Department, Andrews and McMeel, 4520 Main Street, Kansas City, Missouri 64111

SUCCESS AFTER

40

LATE BLOOMERS WHO MADE IT BIG

— DEDICATION —

To my good and trusted friend Bruce Nash, who dreamed during the first forty years of his life what he's now living in the prime of his life.

— Allan Zullo

To the memory of my mother Mary, and to "The Chief," my father William.

— Bill Hartigan

We wish to thank Stephanie Osowski of *Entrepreneur Magazine* for her assistance.

— Contents —

So, What Are You Going to Do with the Rest of Your Life?

You've stumbled past the magic age of forty. Say, weren't you supposed to be heading the marketing department by now? Or running your own upscale boutique? Or writing that best-selling thriller? At the very least, weren't you supposed to know by now what you want to do with the rest of your life?

Okay, so you're not where you thought you'd be now that you're over forty. No need to panic. Midlife status does not mean midlife crisis. Actually, it holds more promise than you think. In fact, this could be the best time to bust loose and fulfill yourself; a chance to change your life.

You can hit your stride at midlife, not hit the wall. You can be burning bright, not burning out. You can be psyched up, not psyched out.

Success after Forty

Many successful people waited until after forty to begin realizing their long-suppressed dreams and independent visions. See for yourself by taking a little spin around the neighborhood: Hop into your Ford and drive to Wal-Mart. At the store, pick up a Gillette razor and a Pepperidge Farm treat. Then grab a bite at McDonald's or Kentucky Fried Chicken. Afterward, better visit Weight Watchers. Finally, pick up your friend at the Mary Kay Cosmetics party. Guess what? All those businesses and products were created by people *after* they reached their fortieth birthday.

That's what this book is all about. It's a collection of inspiring stories of men and women from all walks of life who, at the age of forty, had yet to even start down the road which ultimately led them to success. This book is not about achievers who climbed clearly marked rungs on corporate ladders, but about risk-takers and dreamers and visionaries who shunned convention to go their own way at midlife.

Some of these profiles are success stories from the '90s;

others are from recent history. You've undoubtedly heard some of these accounts before, but they're worth another look. They all serve as a reminder of the remarkable potential that exists in each of us as we enter into the second half of our lives.

You'll discover that although the achievers' stories may be unique, the secrets of their successes are pretty basic. They reached their goals by filling a need, following their hearts, turning failure into opportunity, chasing after their dreams, refusing to give up, or bringing their vision to life.

These successful midlifers may have taken different paths and relied on different methods to reach their goals, but they all shared certain traits: They possessed a strong sense of purpose. They radiated great passion. And, perhaps most important of all, they believed in themselves and what they were doing—even when few others did.

Who would believe an overweight, ex-boxer-turned-preacher could recapture the title of heavyweight champion of the world at age forty-five? George Foreman did—and then went out and proved it.

Who would believe a forty-eight-year-old widow who had never owned a business before could start her own cosmetics company and turn it into a billion-dollar enterprise? Mary Kay Ash did—and then went out and proved it.

Are you pushing fifty or even sixty? So what? There's still plenty of time to find success. Ray Kroc was a fifty-two-year-old traveling salesman of milk shake mixers before he launched McDonald's. Harland Sanders was sixty-five before he began selling his Kentucky Fried Chicken franchises from his car.

The younger generation does not have a monopoly on fresh new thoughts or dreams or visions. Often great ideas become great only because they were spawned from years of experience and practical knowledge. Sam Walton opened his first Wal-Mart at age forty-four. Henry Ford launched the Ford Motor Company at age forty.

Don't think for a moment that because you've suffered

some setbacks at midlife all hope is lost of ever finding success. During his forties, Abraham Lincoln was twice defeated in runs for the Senate and lost his bid for his party's vice presidential nomination. Yet the next time he threw his hat into the political arena, he wound up president of the United States.

Sure, times are different today, but the human spirit isn't. It's ageless. So is persistence and ambition and imagination. And hope.

Many of us baby boomers have been on the fast track so long we've lost sight of why we are running or even where we are headed. Too often where we're headed is toward a career crash. Layoffs, firings, bankruptcies, buyouts, and downsizing have all smashed dreams and plans like a freeway pileup. Achievers may lose their jobs, get rejected, watch their companies fail, or see their ideas founder. But they take advantage of adversity, carving new opportunities and new ventures when they are well beyond the age of forty.

Success after Forty

Midlife is a time to show that if you're persistent, you can succeed where smarter and more talented people fail; that if you learn from the past, you gain strength in the future; if you find what you do best, the best will be found in you. The people profiled in this book prove that midlife can be a thriving period of creativity, growth, and opportunity—and not a time of "pompous mediocrity," as some unenlightened scribe once labeled it, and as too many boomers wrongly believe.

"I remember now that the toughest birthday I ever faced was my fortieth," said writer-director Norman Corwin when he was eighty-two. "It was a big symbol because it said good-bye, good-bye, good-bye to youth. But I think that when one has passed through that age, it's like breaking the sound barrier."

It's not too late to create your own sonic boom—and find success after forty.

Nothing splendid has ever been achieved except by those who dared believe that something inside them was superior to circumstance.

— Bruce Barton

Harvey Tauman

Nothing could shake Harvey Tauman from believing he would be a big success. Despite years of disappointment, he refused to waver from his belief that he was following the right path toward his goal. He just didn't realize how long it would take to get there.

When Tauman was growing up in New York, he took an active interest in

> *"It doesn't matter what your age. Just keep your eye on your dream and never, never let anything distract you."*

the stock market, buying his first stock at age twelve. He hoped to one day head a public company in the health business. After graduating from high school in 1958, he went to work for his father's two-man dental lab and helped expand it into one of the country's largest dental laboratories, with over 250 technicians.

In 1965, when he was twenty-four, Tauman, an avid reader of scientific journals, saw an article about a Czechoslovakian who developed a water-attracting polymer. Convinced that the polymer could be used in oral health and other consumer applications, Tauman began acquiring the rights to it. In 1970 he took his company, Dento-Med, public, moved it to Florida, and changed its focus to research and development for new uses of the polymer, which he now called Hydron.

One day, his wife, Ilene, suggested that the water-attracting and water-retaining polymer might work wonders in skin care. Tauman then embarked on a lengthy and costly search to find a way to put Hydron in creams and lotions.

"Once I believed in the product, that's all it took," Tauman said. "I had a simple formula: one little step at a time. Nothing would change my belief. They say, 'Keep your eye on the light at the end of the tunnel.' I did." But that light looked awfully dim, and the tunnel awfully long.

"It was incredible," Tauman recalled. "We struggled plenty for years and years and years. We had one car in the family and we made bread every week. We were just surviving. In those early years, the company was selling a dental product made of Hydron. We were doing about $100,000 in sales a year and spending about $2 million a year on research."

Tauman refused to give up on his idea of Hydron cosmetics and kept convincing investors and shareholders to pour more money into the profitless company. "Literally every penny that I had, I put in the company to keep it going," he said. "That's how we struggled through the difficult years. I didn't know how long it was going to take. All I knew was that we would do it. There was never a doubt in my mind."

By 1981, Tauman was forty years old. His company, now in Boca Raton, Florida, remained unprofitable and wasn't showing much promise. "We were still suffering big time, trying to make commercial products out of this material."

Success after Forty

Tauman had hired two top chemists who told him it was impossible to form a stable, cosmetically appealing emulsion containing the Hydron polymer. "That made me more anxious and dedicated to making it work," said Tauman. "I told them to keep trying."

Finally in 1989, when he was forty-eight, Tauman received the news he had longed to hear. The chemists had found a way to make Hydron work in skin cream. Dento-Med, which was quickly granted U.S. and international patents on its Hydron emulsion technology, began making Hydron Plus Hand & Body Moisturizer.

"I didn't feel any relief yet," Tauman recalled. "The next thing we had to do was find a way to take these products to market and earn money on them." Unfortunately, he had little marketing experience, no sales staff, no distribution network, and no brand identity.

In 1993—the twenty-third straight year that the company had reported a loss—the fifty-two-year-old Tauman approached the QVC television shopping network. QVC offered him fifteen minutes of live airtime to sell Hydron. If the product sold well, QVC would bring it back. If not, Hydron was history.

Achievers by Persistence

QVC wanted Tauman, who had no television or public speaking experience, to make the pitch in front of the cameras. "I was always afraid to talk in front of people," recalled Tauman. "But QVC said it was either me or nobody because no one believed in the product like I did. I was so nervous because I wanted to succeed. I had no idea what I was going to say."

After all the years, all the struggle, all the red ink, Harvey Tauman's greatest opportunity was at hand. This was his biggest opportunity ever to succeed. He just had to do well. To flop now would be devastating to the company and to the long-suffering shareholders. The pressure on Tauman was enormous. Despite his nervousness, he fought off any negative thoughts.

Answering questions from QVC hostess Jane Rudolph Treacy, Tauman spoke from the heart about Hydron. Ten minutes later, the producer stopped the segment. "I didn't know what had happened," Tauman recalled. "I thought something was wrong. Then they told me they always stop the segment whenever their inventory of the product is sold. They said, 'Harvey, you sold out. People believed you. They really love you.' Coming off the stage, I had tears in my eyes."

Success after Forty

At the most critical point in his company's life, Tauman's performance gave Hydron the boost it needed to soar into orbit. QVC brought Tauman back ten more times that year to sell Hydron, each appearance bringing ever-increasing sales. Once, Tauman sold $236,000 of the $13.25 item in only twelve minutes. Another time, more than $2.4 million in Hydron retail sales was racked up on QVC in a twenty-four-hour period.

With its growing success, Dento-Med changed its name to Hydron Technologies in 1993 and developed new skin care products. The company and QVC then signed an exclusive licensing agreement making the electronic retailer the sole distributor of Hydron-based consumer products in the Western Hemisphere.

In 1994, Hydron Technologies introduced facial moisturizers, cleansers, toner, alpha-hydroxy acid treatment, and eye cream. During one hour-long QVC segment with "Hydron Harvey," the products generated a then-record $800,000 in retail sales. Later that year, QVC began pitching the products on TV throughout Europe.

"There's no question that my belief in Hydron took it to the point of becoming a reality," said Tauman. "And now the products sell by themselves. I truly believe that Hydron will be one of the most profitable, multi-billion-dollar companies you will ever see."

In January 1995, after more than two decades, Hydron Technologies announced its first quarterly profit. "Within twenty-four hours of reporting our first profit, I declared our first cash dividend to our shareholders," said Tauman. "That was a proud moment. That was exciting for me to do."

Reflecting on his struggle to succeed, the millionaire said, "If I would've worried about more than just the development of my product, I never would have made it. I never doubted the monies would be there. I just focused on achieving our objectives. I wouldn't give strength to anything negative or allow a negative thought to get into my brain. Anybody who tried that, I wouldn't talk to them. I knew that I had to give 100 percent of my concentration to what we were doing."

When asked to give advice for anyone over forty who has yet to act on his or her dream, Tauman said, "I don't believe age means anything. Experience can help. But not always. Someone once said that if I had gone to college, I never would have achieved what I did because I would have been taught that we couldn't do the things we ended up doing.

Success after Forty

"You must make sure you know what you're doing, that you have some evidence you are right. You can't just go into something wild and hope for the best. Once you know, you must allow nothing negative to enter the thought process.

"You are going to get tripped up. You are going to get hurt. But don't take your eyes off the light at the end of the tunnel. You have to be exceedingly strong-willed. You must shut off the rest of the world.

"Focus and accomplish, that's all there is to it."

Harland Sanders

When he was fifteen years old, Indiana-born, grade-school drop-out Harland Sanders embarked on a twenty-five-year career of one low-paying job after another. Farmhand, buggy painter, streetcar conductor, plowman, ferryboat operator, insurance salesman, railroad laborer.

But even in his most miserable moments, when he was making sixteen cents an hour driving spikes and unloading coal cars for pennies, Sanders kept plugging away. He never quit believing that success was just around the corner. Year after year, he worked hard, but things never seemed to work out for him in a big way.

Always trying to better himself, Sanders took a correspondence course in law that eventually earned him a doctor of law degree from Southern University. It enabled him to practice in the justice of the peace

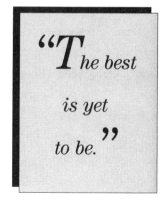

"The best is yet to be."

courts in Little Rock, Arkansas. But he didn't make much money from law.

Throughout this work odyssey, Sanders improved the culinary skills that he had been developing since his teenage days.

But over the years he gave no thought to using those talents for profit. The idea first occurred to him in 1929 when he was thirty-nine years old, shortly after he had opened a service station in Corbin, Kentucky. When a traveling salesman complained that there was no decent place to eat in town, Sanders agreed.

The remark stuck in Sanders's mind and he decided that the problem presented an opportunity. No one, least of all Harland Sanders, realized then that the seeds had been planted for America's fast-food revolution.

"I got to thinking about it, don't you see, and it came to me that one thing I always could do was cook," Sanders told his biographer, John Ed Pearce. "I figured I couldn't do worse than these people running these places around town."

So Sanders fixed up his 12-by-15-foot storage room in the back of the service station and turned it into a dining room to feed the occasional hungry traveler on the side.

Achievers by Persistence

His specialties were the southern-style dishes he had learned from his mother—pan-fried chicken, country ham, fresh vegetables, and home-made biscuits. Slowly the delectable food at the Sanders place gained a reputation, and finally the demand for his cooking became so great that he closed the gas station and opened a restaurant called Sanders Cafe. He was forty-two years old.

Encouraged in the late 1930s by an endorsement from the influential food critic Duncan Hines in his *Adventures in Good Eating*, Sanders enlarged the café. It soon seated 142 patrons, but retained the homelike atmosphere. He also took an eight-week course in restaurant and hotel management at Cornell University so he could be a better restaurateur.

Fried chicken was a Sanders staple. But pan-frying was slow, and deep-fat frying was unsuitable because it produced a chicken that did not meet the Colonel's exacting standards.

In 1939, when Sanders was forty-nine, he discovered the ideal method of cooking chicken with the aid of a new invention called the pressure cooker. In less than ten minutes, the pressure cooker delivered a chicken that retained flavor and moisture. It had an excellent finish, not oily or crusty.

Success after Forty

But Sanders was still seeking ways to improve his chicken. He experimented with seasonings until he created what he thought was the perfect blend of herbs and spices.

Business was better than ever. But in 1940 when Sanders turned fifty, he confided to friends that he had not achieved what he had hoped to accomplish by that age. He felt time was slipping away from him.

"Sanders didn't just daydream," recalled friend John Y. Brown Sr. "His dreams ate him up. He wanted to be a big man, looked up to." And though Sanders was moderately successful on a local level, he felt he hadn't come close to reaching his definition of success. He kept plugging away.

In 1949, the fifty-nine-year-old restaurateur was presented with a Kentucky colonel's commission by the governor's office. It changed his life. Instead of being businessman Harland Sanders, he was now Colonel Harland Sanders. He even looked the part—long, flowing white hair, a goatee and mustache bleached white, white linen suit, white shirt, black string tie, and black shoes. He called himself Colonel and signed his name that way. The persona was good for business, he thought.

In 1953, Sanders was offered $164,000 for his business. Although tempted, he turned it down. He assumed there would be an interchange between the new I-75 and U.S. 25, which ran past his restaurant. But three years later, he was shocked to learn that U.S. 25 was being rerouted. It would no longer run past his business. He was forced to sell his restaurant at auction for just $75,000, barely enough to clear his debts.

With his clientele gone, the Colonel was faced with the prospect of trying to retire on his savings and his Social Security. He was almost sixty-six years old. His first Social Security check was for $105—a paltry sum he knew wouldn't carry his wife and him very far. Once more, he was down. But he was not out.

"The wonderful thing about the Colonel is that he never thought of quitting," said John Y. Brown Jr., who would later own Kentucky Fried Chicken. "When he got that first check, he sat down and . . . said to himself, 'Now, by God, there's something in this world I can do better than anyone else. And the only thing I can think of is frying chicken, so that's what I'll do.'"

A year earlier, Sanders had sold his chicken recipe on a franchise basis to a Utah restaurateur who had done very well with it. Impressed by that success, a few other owners had agreed to pay Sanders four cents for every chicken they cooked with his process. Sanders now figured that other restaurant owners might be interested in such an arrangement.

The Colonel loaded a few pressure cookers and packages of his secret herbs and spices into the trunk of his white Cadillac and hit the road. Despite his age and his painful arthritis, Sanders told himself that he could—and would—make one more stab at big-time success.

"Hell," he later said, "I had to."

He would drive to a restaurant and offer to cook his chicken for the manager and employees. If they liked it, he would spend a few days there cooking chicken for the customers. If they liked it, he would make an informal agreement with the owner on the same basis as his early contracts: four cents per chicken cooked Sanders-style.

Wrote biographer John Ed Pearce, "Colonel Sanders had spent nearly a half century selling, and he knew that, regardless of the product at the moment, what he was really selling was himself. He knew that he had enough self-confidence, a belief in his ability to perform his role. He believed deeply in his product. But there were moments, during those first months on the road, when he had to fight back the gnawing pangs of doubt."

Achievers by Persistence

Day after day, he drove the dreary midwestern roads looking for restaurants where the owners could see the future of Kentucky Fried Chicken. Often, he slept in the backseat of his car to save the cost of a motel. He would shave in the restroom of a service station and stare in the mirror and give himself a pep talk.

In the first two years of travel, Sanders collected a grand total of five franchises. He later explained, "When you tell a restaurant man his chicken isn't as good as it ought to be, it usually insults him." But good cooking eventually triumphed.

By 1960, when he was seventy years old, there were more than 200 Kentucky Fried Chicken outlets in the United States and Canada. The Colonel had stopped traveling, allowing the franchise inquiries to come to him. He did his own bookkeeping and his wife Claudia mixed and mailed the blend of spices.

By 1963, the popularity of Kentucky Fried Chicken—now with more than six hundred outlets—was too much for the Colonel to handle, even with the help of his wife and 167 employees who worked in a building behind his house.

Success after Forty

He sold the franchise business to marketing maven John Y. Brown Jr. and Nashville millionaire Jack Massey for $2 million and a lifetime salary of $40,000 (later raised to $75,000) for advisory and publicity work and a seat on the board of directors. In 1971, seven years after the sale, the number of franchises rose to 3,500 before it was bought by Heublein, Inc. In 1995, Kentucky Fried Chicken had 9,400 outlets and reported sales of seven billion dollars.

One of Brown's cleverest moves was the promotion of Colonel Sanders's image. Realizing that the quirky rags-to-riches Sanders was a unique asset, Brown hired a publicity agent and set out to make the Colonel one of the best-known personalities in the United States. In thousands of appearances at stores, fairs, and on television, the six-foot, two-hundred-pound Colonel charmed millions with his southern courtesy and crotchety personality. Aided by the Colonel's indefatigability and his willingness to travel hundreds of thousands of miles a year, the promotional campaign created a living symbol for KFC—and proved that age was no barrier to success.

When members of Congress asked Sanders what one should do to prepare for retirement, the Colonel replied, "Give him an opportunity to do for himself. Never stop working! A man will rust out before he wears out."

In 1980, at the age of ninety, Colonel Sanders died.

"His life is an inspiration," said Brown. "It is proof that the Great American Dream still exists, that if you have a better idea, the imagination to sell it, and the will to outwork the competition, it is still possible to achieve great things."

Sanders's life should be a constant reminder that no matter how old you are, "the best is yet to be," as the Colonel often said.

To Pearce, Sanders was a man of indomitable courage. "If we seek the genius of Harland Sanders, we will find it in the fact that he would not be conquered. No matter how often or how brutally life knocked him down, he rose to his feet once more, staggering and bloody perhaps, but determined to stand and try once more. He was unusual in that he would not recognize defeat. He succeeded mainly because he refused to fail."

Alex Haley

To millions of readers, *Roots* was a stunning, poignant reaffirmation of the black heritage. To its author, it was a triumph of faith and perseverance.

Alex Haley's search for his African ancestry began when he was a child in Henning, Tennessee. On summer afternoons, he would listen intently as his grandmother, Cynthia Palmer, and other relatives gathered on the front porch and traded lively, dramatic stories of their family history.

To the young boy's delight, he learned about Uncle Mingo, Massa Walker, Miss Kizzy, Tom, and Chicken George. Alex also was enthralled by accounts of Toby, who had been captured into slavery as a young boy in Africa.

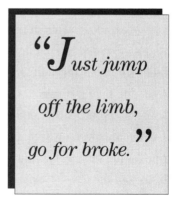

"*Just jump off the limb, go for broke.*"

Success after Forty

Alex promised himself that one day he would tell those fascinating stories as well as his relatives did.

Growing up in southern towns where his father Simon taught in black colleges, Haley discovered a love for reading. He finished high school two years early and went to college. But he quit at the age of seventeen and enlisted in the Coast Guard.

Because he was a skilled typist, Haley brought a portable typewriter with him on board ship. He began ghosting love letters for the crew to their girlfriends.

Haley also wrote sensationalized love stories. Every time he landed in port, he would mail his stories to *True Confessions* and *Modern Romances*. As Haley would later admit, the stories were dreadful and every one of them had been rejected by the magazines' editors. In fact, he received over one hundred rejection letters over an eight-year period before he sold his first article, a nonfiction piece about the Coast Guard.

Eventually, he was stationed in New York in a public relations position for the service. He continued to write and soon sold stories about the history of the Coast Guard to *Coronet* magazine. More than anything, he wanted to be a full-time writer just as soon as he completed his twenty years in the service. In the meantime, he planned to spend every spare moment writing, making contacts, and peddling his work.

In 1959, at the age of thirty-eight, Haley left the Coast Guard and went looking for steady work in public relations. "I wanted to make it as a writer, but I turned chicken and came to New York to find a job," he recalled. He sent out twenty-five résumés to the city's biggest advertising and public relations agencies and put his photo on every résumé. Only two responded. No one bothered to even interview him.

"I decided to make it as a writer or else," he recalled. "Just jump off the limb, go for broke. I guess I wrote sixteen to eighteen hours a day for seven days a week."

Haley found the cheapest accommodations available—a dark, one-room basement apartment in Greenwich Village—and prepared to starve. "One day I was down to eighteen cents and a couple of cans of sardines, and that was it," he recalled.

Broke and discouraged, Haley sought friendship and support from other local black writers whose work he admired. He wrote to six of them asking for advice and encouragement. The only one to respond was James Baldwin, the highly respected author of *Go Tell It on the Mountain*. "[Baldwin], who didn't know me from Adam, came right over and spent hours talking to me, cheering me up," said Haley. "I've never forgotten that."

Haley was determined to keep working toward his goal of becoming a well-known—and well-compensated—author, no matter how bad things looked at the time. He believed that if one worked hard enough and long enough at something, eventually an opportunity would come along.

In 1960, when he was thirty-nine, Haley wrote his first important article after interviewing Black Muslim leader Malcolm X for *Reader's Digest*. The honest profile of the controversial figure showed Haley's gifts as a writer and interviewer.

Two years later *Playboy* invited him to do a series of interviews with infamous personalities. Among those he profiled was American Nazi leader George Lincoln Rockwell—who held a gun on Haley throughout their conversation.

In 1963, when Haley was forty-two, Malcolm X asked the writer to help him with his autobiography. Haley spent a year interviewing the Muslim leader and another year writing the book. *The Autobiography of Malcolm X* received critical acclaim and sold more than six million copies in eight languages. (Malcolm X, who was Haley's good friend, was murdered by assassins shortly before the manuscript was submitted to the publisher.)

Instead of celebrating his own success, the forty-four-year-old writer took the time to examine his life and his career. Over the years, he had become a master at telling other people's stories, not his own. It was time to work on a more personal project—the rise of his grandmother's family from slavery to his own childhood in Tennessee. Doubleday gave him a five thousand dollar advance for the book, which he planned to call *Before This Anger.*

The advance wasn't nearly enough money to cover expenses, so he continued to write magazine articles while he worked on the book, which he thought would take only a couple of years to complete.

He sifted through endless record files, registries, and rolls of microfilm at dozens of libraries, archives, and record halls around the country. To his delight, he was able to confirm the identities of his early ancestors that he had heard so much about in his grandmother's stories.

Success after Forty

In early 1966, Haley felt he was ready to begin writing the book. But to complete this story, he knew he would have to go to Africa and learn what he could about his ancestor Toby—the slave born in Africa as Kunta Kinte.

Haley traveled to Gambia where he discovered the *griots*, old African storytellers. They each had learned the entire history of families and could recite from memory births, deaths, marriages, and stories of important people dating hundreds of years into the past. In a tiny remote village, thousands of miles away from home, Haley was astounded when he met a *griot* who knew the complete story about the early life of Kunta Kinte—Haley's great-great-great-great-grandfather.

When it became clear that Haley was Kinte's descendant, the villagers surrounded the author in a ceremonial dance, embraced him as one of their own, and prayed over him as a long-lost son.

Wrote Haley's biographer David Shirley, "Haley now realized that he had found an entire race of people to whom he was bound, not merely by name and by blood, but by a common history of suffering and loss. Millions of other men, women, and children had been hauled in chains across the Atlantic Ocean during the early days of America's history or had died during the cruel months at sea. And millions more, he now realized, had been left behind in their African homeland, robbed of their parents and children, their brothers and their sisters.

"He thought of all those nameless, faceless others who had suffered and died in silence, apart from their homes, their language, and those they loved—and with no one to tell their story. It was a story he was resolved to reveal."

What had once been a modestly conceived family memoir had now expanded to epic proportions. However, Haley was faced with some harsh realities. He needed years of more research. Where would he raise the tens of thousands of dollars to fund it? How would he ever find the time and energy to finish such a book? What toll would it take on his family?

Here he was, a forty-six-year-old man in his second marriage who needed to dedicate perhaps another eight to ten years to a project that held no promise—except in his heart—of being successful. To Haley, there was no choice. He felt it was his destiny to flesh out and authenticate Kunta Kinte's life and those of Kinte's descendants.

Success after Forty

Haley's research became obsessive and detailed. To portray effectively the terrors confronting Kinte on the slave ship *Lord Ligonier*, Haley booked passage on a freighter sailing from West Africa to the United States. Each night of the ten-day voyage, he went down to the dark, cold hold where he stripped to his underwear. Recalled Haley, "I lay on my back on a wide, rough, bare dunnage plank and forced myself to stay there through all ten nights of the crossing, trying to imagine what did he see, hear, feel, smell, taste—and above all, in knowing Kunta, what things did he think?"

Haley felt he had earned the right to describe Kinte's suffering. Haley was suffering too, in other ways. Debts, the impatience of his publisher, and the prospect of boiling a decade's research into a readable manuscript led Haley to the ship's stern one night. There, he thought of jumping overboard. "All I'd have to have done was step between the rails," he said. "It would be a very private act, and a relatively painless one. Nobody would know until the next morning." But his commitment to finish what he started and the sense of generations of his family watching over him helped hold him back.

Achievers by Persistence

For the next eight years, Haley balanced the time he spent researching and writing the book with a breathless schedule of interviews, lectures, and public appearances around the country to help keep him financially afloat.

By the time the project was completed, Haley had spent eighty- thousand dollars, traveled a half-million miles, talked with thousands of people, studied untold numbers of records, and visited more than fifty libraries and archives on three continents.

In 1976, at the age of fifty-five, Haley's perseverance paid off. His all-consuming project *Roots* finally was published—to great fanfare. For Haley, it meant fame and fortune.

More than eight million copies of the book were sold worldwide in thirty-one languages. Haley became one of the best-known and most highly celebrated writers in the world. A Roper poll conducted at the time found Haley to be the third most admired black man in America.

He received almost three hundred awards, special citations, and honorary degrees for his work on *Roots*. But the greatest honor of all came in April 1977 when Haley was awarded a special Pulitzer Prize—one of the most prestigious literary awards in America. The Pulitzer Committee said his ground-breaking epic was an "important contribution to the history of slavery."

That same year, *Roots* was turned into the most-watched dramatic series in television history at the time. More than one hundred million viewers saw the concluding episode of the eight-part series. (As of 1995, the finale ranked as the third-most-watched program; while four other *Roots* episodes remain in the top thirty of all time.) In 1978, ABC produced and aired a sequel, *Roots: The Next Generations*, featuring an even larger and more distinguished cast than the original. James Earl Jones portrayed Haley.

Said the proud author, who died in 1992 at the age of seventy, "I find myself looking at the book as I imagine a mother who has held her baby on her lap might feel watching him take his first steps."

Morgan Freeman

Morgan Freeman arrived late to stardom. He might never have arrived had he not been surrounded by those who believed in him so much that he knew he could never give up.

For decades, his career as a New York actor was a stop-and-go journey of critically praised stage performances and long stretches of unemployment. Time and again he flirted with the thought of quitting—but his friends wouldn't let him. And neither would his heart.

Despite the periods of no work, Freeman kept at his craft because he loved it so much. Not until he reached his fifties did Freeman finally become a movie star—and a three-time Oscar nominee.

> *"You can't give up. You're not allowed to give up."*

Success after Forty

The road to success was a long one. Born in Memphis in 1937, Freeman came from a broken home and spent part of his youth in the street-gang world of Chicago's South Side. "My gang was called the Spiders," he recalled. "I was never really a full-fledged member, but I was stealing and conning all the same."

He took refuge from his warlike surroundings in the classroom. "School was the one place I could shine, so I always went to class," he said.

In 1948, when he was eleven, his family settled in Greenwood, Mississippi, where he developed a fondness for movies. He collected milk and soda bottles and used the deposit money to buy movie tickets. "I went to the movies every day. My heroes were Gary Cooper and Spencer Tracy. They portrayed quiet men with dignity."

Early in life, Freeman learned that people believed in him—especially his teachers, who encouraged him to take up drama. "When a teacher tells you that you're going to make it, that you've got what it takes, all you can do is keep going," he said.

At age twelve, he won a statewide drama competition and later had his own radio show in high school. "I was ambitious, but it was not a recognizable ambition to act," he said. "It was an ambition to do something."

After high school and a stint in the Air Force as a radar mechanic, Freeman headed for Hollywood, expecting to take the town by storm. His first stop was Paramount. "I thought I'd just present myself and be hired," he recalled.

"It was like 'Okay, everybody, I'm here!' And it was a real jolt because not only did people not know who I was, but they didn't care. And I was certain they were all lined up, waiting for me." Instead, he learned a bitter truth—roles for black actors in the late 1950s were rare.

So he worked as a transcript clerk at Los Angeles City College, where he took acting, voice, and diction lessons on the side. A year later, he drove to New York looking for acting jobs. Over the next few years, between auditions and bit stage roles, he tried to survive by taking odd jobs.

He was a dancer at the 1964 World's Fair and a counterman at a carry-out shop in Penn Station. "I washed cars, sold ads for a black magazine, and worked at the post office," he recalled. "I bummed a lot and lived on quarter-pound Baby Ruths for dinner." He lived the painful life of a struggling actor, but he wasn't about to give up yet.

Success after Forty

In 1965, at the age of twenty-eight, Freeman landed his first film role in *The Pawnbroker*—as an extra. But at least it was work. "It doesn't matter at what level you're doing it if you're being paid to be a professional," he said. "I thought, 'I'm here! I made it! I'm doing it!' That kept me going through all the ups and downs."

During the downs, Freeman lost faith in himself many times, he admitted. But that's when friends stepped in. "They were there to say, 'You can't give up. You're not allowed to give up.'"

One time, Freeman failed to persuade a friend to give him an office job to make ends meet. Freeman was angered until he realized that his friend was really trying to help him. If his friend believed in Freeman's acting ability, Freeman thought, then he should too. "I was pushed toward what I really wanted to do," Freeman said. "Everything else was just a fallback. Ultimately, I realized that 'falling back' is not something you should prepare for."

Belief in himself grew stronger in 1966 while he was in the chorus of a touring company of *The Royal Hunt of the Sun*. When one of the lead actors collapsed onstage, Freeman took over the role because he was the understudy. Recalled Freeman, "It was like 'Yeah! This is right! Acting! That's what I'm supposed to be doing.'"

Over the next few years, he received excellent notices from the critics for his stage performances throughout the northeast.

Meanwhile, in 1971, the thirty-four-year-old Freeman joined the cast of *The Electric Company*, a new PBS TV show designed to improve children's reading skills through songs and skits. As Easy Reader, Freeman played a hip disc jockey who celebrated the joys of reading.

Ironically, having a steady job caused him anguish and torment. He found the work monotonous and unchallenging.

"It was a terrific opportunity, but I was also stuck on a television series, trying to come to terms with being Easy Reader for the rest of my life," he recalled. "I was too insecure to quit. I was trapped in a job that I meant to do for a couple of years. Five years later, I was still waking up to the same 9-to-5 gig."

Although Freeman appreciated the steady income that the show provided, he grew tired of the role after two years. He turned to the bottle for solace.

Success after Forty

"I was drinking too much and before I knew it, it got out of control," he said. "Next thing I knew, I was going through two or three quarts of whiskey a week, which . . . was too much for me. I remember waking up once in my doorway, where I had fallen down. And I lay there thinking, 'You're lying face down, drunk, and this will never do.' And so I quit drinking."

When the series ended in 1976, so did his first marriage. He blamed it on alcohol abuse. Eventually Freeman found a new resolve and a new wife, costume designer Myrna Colley-Lee.

In 1978, at the age of forty-one, he started getting noticed as a gifted actor after his performance in the Broadway play *The Mighty Gents*. It's the story of four former members of a street gang trying to survive in the adult world. He received spectacular reviews and earned a Tony nomination and other accolades. Unfortunately, the show closed after only nine performances.

Awards and glowing reviews were nice, but they didn't put food on the table. "The press comes around and tells you that you're the greatest thing since smoked sausage," he said. "But none of that translates into something you can give your landlord or grocer or your cleaner.

Achievers by Persistence

"Even though I was voted Most Promising Newcomer [after *Mighty Gents*], I couldn't get another job. The phone stopped ringing, and I was seriously considering driving a taxi."

Freeman was a forty-six-year-old out-of-work actor wondering where his life was headed. Although he mulled over other options, he knew he couldn't quit. Acting was his life.

Then he snared the leading role in a touring production of *The Gospel at Colonus*, a musical fusion of a Greek tragedy and a black Pentecostal church service. His electrifying performance earned him an Obie in 1984.

In 1987, at the age of fifty, Freeman starred in the Off-Broadway play *Driving Miss Daisy*, portraying Hoke Colburn, an aging chauffeur for an elderly Jewish widow in Atlanta in the 1950s. Again he received rave reviews.

Although he had done a few bit parts in the movies, no one in the film industry paid much attention to him—until he was cast as the violent but charismatic pimp Fast Black in the little-seen 1987 film *Street Smart*. Freeman delivered a stunning performance that stood out all the more because the film was a box-office disaster. But the critics took notice and so did his colleagues. Freeman was nominated for an Oscar as Best Supporting Actor.

His movie career began to soar. His first starring role was in 1989 in *Lean on Me*, the true-life story of Joe Clark, a no-nonsense high school principal. Although the film received mixed notices, critics hailed Freeman.

He finally achieved recognition from moviegoers when he reprised his role of Hoke in the film adaptation of *Driving Miss Daisy*, which won the Academy Award for Best Picture and brought Freeman his second Oscar nomination.

"I just sort of had a visceral understanding of who Hoke was," said Freeman. "I grew up with people like him in Mississippi. He came from my own background. Giving life to that man was a labor of love—a true labor of love. That was more important than the success he brought me."

Because of his remarkable performance, the Hollywood establishment bestowed upon the actor the credibility he had worked so hard to achieve. He was no longer another working actor with a long résumé. He was now a name, a star.

Morgan Freeman had arrived.

In 1995—just six years after he first became a movie star—the fifty-

Achievers by Persistence

eight-year-old actor got his third Oscar nod for his portrayal of a veteran prisoner in *The Shawshank Redemption*. The years of Baby Ruth dinners, unemployment lines, and odd jobs were now history—but not forgotten.

"The suffering is over," he told the *New York Daily News*. "I've suffered trying to get here and be successful. Once you take the initial plunge into success, you just settle back and say, 'Okay, I can do this.'"

Thanks to Freeman's success, he has a home in Manhattan, a pricey sailboat in the Virgin Islands, and a farm in Charleston, Mississippi, where he raises horses.

"I guess I've always fantasized," he said. "I've always dreamed big dreams. I wasn't always sure they'd come true." Now he's living the dream. "The question is, what are you dreaming of next?

"Once you have fame and success, you don't want to spend the rest of your life worrying if you're going to lose it. Fame isn't what you want, really. Stardom isn't what you want. What you really want is to work at something that you care about. People say to me, 'Well, Morgan, you finally made it.' And I say, 'No, I made it the first time I got the chance to tread the boards on a stage with the boys in New York City.'"

— Pursuers of Visions —

We must have courage to bet on our ideas,
to take the calculated risk, and to act.

— Maxwell Maltz

Sam Walton

As the owner of retail stores in the South, Sam Walton could have said, "I've had enough," and sold out and enjoyed a comfortable life by age forty. But that wasn't Walton's style. He had some unfinished business—to follow through on a challenging vision. All his life, he saw beyond the present, always innovating, experimenting, expanding,

> *"Believe in your idea even when maybe some other folks don't, and stick to your guns."*

and learning. He needed to see his vision come to life.

Born in 1918 into a solid family headed by Thomas Walton, a farm-mortgage broker, Sam grew up in Columbia, Missouri, where he excelled in athletics in high school. After graduating from the University of Missouri with a degree in economics, Walton took his first retailing job at a J.C. Penney store in Des Moines, Iowa. Walton met the then sixty-five-year-old John Cash Penney and learned the retailer's principles, including "pack the customer's dollar full of value, quality, and satisfaction." It was sage advice Walton would never forget.

After serving in the army during World War II, Walton struck out on his own by borrowing enough money to open a Ben Franklin variety store in Newport, Arkansas. He built the store into a major success. Unfortunately, he had overlooked one important clause in his lease—renewal of the lease was completely up to the landlord. When the landlord saw how prosperous the store was doing, he refused to renew the lease, forcing Walton to sell the store to the landlord's son.

Walton was thirty-two years old and out of business. "It was the low point of my business life," he recalled. "I felt sick to my stomach. I had built the best variety store in the whole region and worked hard in the community—done everything right—and now I was being kicked out of town. It didn't seem fair. But I didn't dwell on my disappointment. The challenge at hand was simple enough to figure out: I had to pick myself up and get on with it, do it all over again, only even better this time."

Walton moved to Bentonville, Arkansas, where he and his younger brother James became Ben Franklin franchisees. Walton expanded until he controlled fifteen stores in Arkansas and Missouri.

Although he was forty-two and making a comfortable living, he wasn't satisfied. He envisioned a better way of retailing. But relying on his business experience wasn't enough. He needed to learn more.

He traveled throughout the East and Midwest, studying large retail chains such as Korvette, Caldor, Kmart, and Zayre. He noticed that the big discount chains always put their stores in or near large cities in the belief that small towns could not generate enough business to make a large store profitable.

But Walton had a different vision. He was convinced larger stores could thrive in smaller markets. "There was a lot more business in those towns than people ever thought," Walton recalled.

He broached the idea of large discount stores in rural areas to Ben Franklin's management, but they gave him little encouragement. Working sixteen to eighteen hours a day, he decided to make his vision a reality without them. He learned all he could about how to successfully run discount stores. For two years, he prowled New England, studying stores and interviewing executives while playing up his folksy, Arkansas country-boy image.

He was especially intrigued with Kmart's operation. "What I did later was take pieces of it and make our Wal-Mart as much like it as we could," he said. "It was a copying proposition."

In 1962, at the age of forty-four, Walton borrowed against his house and property—and most everything else he had—to go into the discount business. He opened his first Wal-Mart store in Rogers, Arkansas. Two years later, he put up stores in nearby Springdale and Harrison.

"Once we opened that Wal-Mart in Springdale, I knew we were on to something," said Walton. "I knew in my bones it was going to work. But at the time, most folks were pretty skeptical of the whole concept."

One of them was retailing executive David Glass, who would later become the company's CEO. When he came to the grand opening of the Harrison Wal-Mart, he was horrified.

"It was the worst retail store I had ever seen," Glass recalled. "Sam had brought a couple of trucks of watermelons in and stacked them on the sidewalk. He had a donkey ride out in the parking lot. It was 115 degrees, and the watermelons began to pop, and the donkey began to do what donkeys do, and it all mixed together and ran all over the parking lot. And when you went inside the store, the mess just continued, having been tracked in all over the floor. He was a nice fellow, but I wrote him off. It was just terrible."

Admitted Walton, "At the start we were so amateurish. We had our merchandise priced right and it worked in small towns. Kmart just ignored us. They let us stay out here, while we developed and learned our business. If they had jumped us . . . I hate to think of that. But we were protected by our small-town market. Kmart [was] self-satisfied with what they had accomplished. They thought they could roll over everybody. And they woke up one day and found out the world had changed, retailing had changed. They were behind.

Success after Forty

"It turned out that the first big lesson we learned was that there was much, much more business out there in small-town America than anybody, including me, had ever dreamed of."

By the age of forty-eight, Sam was still caught in the throes of business expansion. He had four Wal-Mart discount stores. He knew if he wanted more stores, he had to buy cheaper and hire smarter and more aggressive retail executives. "I have always pursued everything I was interested in with a true passion—some would say obsession—to win," he said. He began building a stronger team.

Walton admitted that he could get "a little tough" whenever he saw things he didn't like. He stressed that he knew his business from bottom to top. "I used to do it all, sweep the floor, keep the books, buy the merchandise. One of my assets is my willingness to try something new, to change. I think that is a concept we carry throughout the company. We have a low resistance to change. We call it our 'RC Factor.'"

The Wal-Mart empire grew slowly but steadily for the next eight years and by 1970—at the age of fifty-two—he owned twenty-five stores. Thirteen years later, the chain had become the eighth largest retailer in the country, with 642 stores in nineteen states and annual sales of over four billion dollars. In that same year, 1983, *Forbes* magazine called Walton the second-richest person in the United States, with a personal fortune of 2.15 billion dollars.

Walton continued to study his competitors assiduously and to underprice them whenever possible. "There aren't many secrets in this industry," he said. "I walked into more competitors' stores than anyone. . . . We learned from everyone else's book and added a few pages of our own." Walton often slipped into rival stores to check their prices on specific items. If the price in any of them was lower than the same item at the local Wal-Mart, he ordered his store manager to reduce the price.

In 1986, *Financial World* named the sixty-eight-year-old Walton "CEO of the Year." Said the magazine:

> The judges were tremendously impressed with the almost compulsive passion he has for his stores, for the people who run them and for his customers. . . . Walton has clearly shown that it is possible to combine the folksiness of a small company with the managerial sophistication of a large one. One judge used words like 'alchemist,' 'wizard,' and 'magician' in characterizing Walton's managerial ability.

Success after Forty

It is no secret that all great CEOs share certain traits. More than just exhibiting self-confidence and a winner's mentality, they have an almost mystical ability to inspire confidence and trust in those around them. The judges found those qualities outstanding in Sam M. Walton.

Under Walton's vision, Wal-Mart, operating in a territory with less than 50 percent of the country's population, went from one billion dollars in sales to one billion dollars in profits in just ten years.

With an estimated net worth of 2.8 billion dollars, Walton reached the top of *Forbes* magazine's list of wealthiest Americans in 1985 when he was sixty-seven. He remained No. 1 on the list through 1991 (when he and his family had a total of 18.5 billion dollars).

"Somewhere out there right now there's someone—probably hundreds of thousands of someones—with good enough ideas to go it all the way," Walton said. "It [business success] will be done again, over and over, providing that someone wants it badly enough to do what it takes to get there."

In March 1992, President George Bush traveled to Wal-Mart's headquarters in Bentonville, Arkansas, to present Sam Walton with the Presidential Medal of Freedom, the federal government's highest civilian award.

Pursuers of Visions

Less than a month later, Sam Walton died. At the time of his death, Wal-Mart—the chain he founded at the age of forty-four—was in forty-three states. By 1995, it was in all fifty states and five countries, and reporting revenues of 82.5 billion dollars.

Said his biographer John Huey, "He was a genius in business, with an iron mind—some said pigheaded—unwilling to compromise any of his carefully thought-out policies and principles. To him, making money was only a game, a test of his imagination and expertise to see how far he could drive a business concept. Wall Street had a hard time getting the drift of that. Sam's idea, he readily admitted, was absurdly simple: Buy cheap. Sell low. Every day. And while doing it, smile!"

Judy George

Judy George never saw anything she did as a failure. If something didn't turn out the way she expected, she viewed it as an opportunity to learn or take action. "I see most things that go wrong as an opportunity—including getting fired," Judy said. "In my case, it forced me to take action on my vision of what a furniture store should be."

In 1974, when all four of her children were in school, Judy, then a thirty-four-year-old housewife from Milton, Massachusetts, started her own business—a decorating and marketing company called Ideas by George. "I felt very guilty about going to work," she recalled. "Like so many others, I felt a woman's primary job is staying home and raising children. I felt I was being selfish by 'abandoning' them."

> "*I* turned my age into a benefit. I had a proven track record, business maturity and experience as a leader—the very things venture capital looks for if they are to invest in your vision."

Success after Forty

Although she was a devoted wife and mother, another part of her belonged to the business world, where she proved quite adept. A year after starting her own firm, Judy was hired to run a division of Hamilton's, a new furniture retailer. After it was bought by Scandinavian Design, she rose through the executive ranks to become president. Although she enjoyed her job, Judy dreamed of creating her own company one day. But she was in no hurry. "I was so in love with my job that I didn't know how to leave," she said.

In 1985, Judy wrote a detailed thirty-page memo describing her vision of where Scandinavian Design should be in the future. She had put her heart and soul into the report. "When I gave it to the CEO, he and his advisers said it was terrible," Judy recalled. "We didn't share the same vision. The CEO felt I was no longer right for the company. I realized I had been living somebody else's dream for the ten years I was with the company. We agreed I should leave."

Suddenly the forty-five-year-old woman found herself out of work. "I felt rejected," she recalled. "I never expected it to happen to me. I felt humiliation, anger, hurt, shame, and every emotion you can imagine—but only for a week. I gave myself time to understand myself so I could be empowered. If I didn't have God, I couldn't have made it through this period. And I couldn't have made it through without having my dream."

Judy turned her failure into an opportunity. "The CEO gave me the push I needed," she said. "I needed to be my own boss, to run things my way, to follow my plans of action. I couldn't do that in someone else's company."

Judy had envisioned a furniture store serving the modern woman, "the cocooning yuppies of the '90s," as she describes them. "They're bright and intelligent, love antiques and art, and read shelter magazines like *House Beautiful*. Fashion is important to them, yet they don't have any definite opinions on the subject. They want to fix up their homes, but aren't quite sure how to get it all together."

While these upwardly-mobile buyers aspire to quality merchandise, they suffer from what Judy calls "furniture frustration." The average customer is treated poorly by uninformed salespeople and by stores that deliver furniture often months late.

When she told her family that she planned to launch her own

company to right these wrongs, they were "scared yet supportive," Judy recalled. She and her husband Simon were a dual-income household by necessity to help pay for three kids in college with another in high school. Judy was forced to take out a second mortgage on her home to finance the planning stages of her company.

Although she had the background and credentials to put her own vision into practice, "it was definitely scary," she admitted. "I was terrified. I found myself on a roller coaster of fear and joy and excitement and challenge and worry."

But Judy also had an enormous ability to capture the moment. "I was let go on July 31 and I had my first meeting with venture capital in September. By the following April, I had all the money in place and tried to hire the best people. I needed to put together a dynamic team of people to execute my vision.

"Fear tends to drive me. Those were scary times, and I was afraid I wouldn't live up to my own expectations. I had to get up every morning and tell myself, 'You will not crack today, no matter what. You are really going to reach your goals today.'"

Pursuers of Visions

During that time, Judy talked to manufacturers about trends and which items were selling best. She surveyed people on their buying habits. She learned what consumers could afford to spend, what types of furniture they liked, and what factors they felt were missing in furniture stores. She also studied window and store displays.

When she put it all together, she had a clear idea of what the market wanted. "I believe in intuitive design," she said. "Everyone has [his or her] own sense of style. Typically, it is an eclectic approach combining different interior design styles. The idea is to help people find the furniture and accessories that tie that style or look together. I intended to help people transform their homes into their own domains.

"The furniture industry is a forty-five-billion-dollar business, dominated by small mom-and-pop stores all over the United States. You have tons of people selling furniture, but nobody had melded fashion and home to come up with an exciting look. And no one had taken the concept and put it in heavily trafficked malls."

Everything was falling in place for Judy. She had the vision, drive, and enthusiasm. And she had a name for her stores—Domain. After persuading four venture capital firms to hand her 3.5 million dollars, the forty-six-year-old mother and wife opened her first Domain store in the Chestnut Hill mall near Boston in 1986.

It was an immediate success. First year sales of Domain totaled five million dollars. She began opening more stores. By 1995, Judy owned twenty stores throughout the northeast as Domain, Inc., recorded sales of fifty million dollars.

Persistence was one of her main recipes for success. "Most people give up too quickly," she said. "When things get painful and stressful, they throw in the towel. Too often, they're just about to turn the corner. If you believe in what you're doing, you should hang in there. You'll be pleasantly surprised when everything falls into place—often when you least expect it.

"I would tell anyone that it's okay to be scared once you take that big step. But if it's a major fear, don't do it. It takes tenacity and staying power to succeed. You must exude confidence, courage, and tenacity.

"You also need to get in touch with what drives you—what you need and what you want. Once I got in touch with who I was and what I needed and wanted, the excitement and passion came out.

Pursuers of Visions

"I didn't worry about my age. In fact, I made it work for me, trading off my experience. And I surrounded myself with people who really liked me and were willing to give me honest feedback. I got rid of all negative thoughts. And then I just worked hard."

As Judy sees it, life is a series of trade-offs. It's just a question of picking the right ones. "Beyond my family, I have practically no personal life," she said. "But that was my choice. Early on, I learned that if you spread yourself too thin, everything you do suffers.

"I didn't just want a job. I wanted to be a leader and build something unique. I love being a mother and a wife, but I also relish the thrill of competing in the work world."

Now a fifty-five-year-old grandmother, Judy George can't imagine not working. "I'm exhilarated by my work. Every day, I get up and I get to go to bat. I don't think of myself as being fifty-five. My work keeps me young."

Henry Ford

Henry Ford never stopped learning, never stopped experimenting, never stopped dreaming. To him, any vision could be brought to life through hard work and thoughtful study.

Born in Dearborn, Michigan, in 1863, Ford grew up on a farm. When he was twelve, he experienced two events that influenced him greatly: He received his first watch and he saw for the first time a horseless vehicle—a road engine used for driving a threshing machine.

When he was thirteen, Ford used crude tools to tinker with fragments of machinery, and built his own watch. A few years later, he had created a working model of the road engine.

At seventeen, he began working at a foundry and machine shop for $2.50 a

> "*Anyone who stops learning is old, whether at twenty or eighty. Anyone who keeps learning stays young. The greatest thing in life is to keep your mind young.*"

week. He supplemented this meager wage with the extra money he earned at night by cleaning and repairing watches.

After reading a magazine article about the recently-invented Otto internal combustion engine, Ford left the machine shop to work for a lower salary at the Dry Dock Engine Company. Two years later, the apprentice had mastered the machinist's trade.

Ford's ambition in those days was to develop a plan for making watches so cheaply that they could be sold for one dollar each. But he gave up his idea because his father needed him. So Ford went home to help with the work on the farm.

However, all of his time wasn't devoted to agriculture. When he was twenty-two, he attended a business college for three months in the winter of 1884–85. He also experimented with machinery in his well-equipped workshop, and in his free time courted Clara Bryant, the daughter of a neighboring farmer, whom he soon married.

Ford became obsessed with machines. After having the opportunity to repair an Otto engine, he was convinced that gas, not steam, would be the driving power of the future.

Pursuers Of Visions

After his marriage, Ford built a home for his wife on a forty-acre wooded tract that his father had given him. There, Ford drew up his first diagram of a gasoline engine. He soon realized he could not build his engine on a farm, but needed the superior mechanical equipment that could only be found in a large city. So in 1891, when he was twenty-eight, he and Clara moved to Detroit, where he found a job as a machinist that paid forty-five dollars a month.

In a small brick shed behind his home, Ford began work on the gasoline engine. It was finished in a week and tested in 1893, when he was thirty, in the Ford kitchen. The engine was clamped to the sink, its spark plug connected to the overhead electric light socket, and Clara tended to the engine's oil cup. To the couple's joy, the engine worked.

Ford's ambition now was to make the engine drive a four-wheel carriage. If he could do it, he thought, then he could make more automobiles and sell them. Although several Europeans had built their own horseless carriages, no one was yet manufacturing motorcars commercially.

Finally, in 1896, at the age of thirty-three, Ford built his first automobile in his backyard shop. There was only one problem. The doorway wasn't big enough. He had to bust a hole in the shop's wall so he could get the vehicle out. Its two-cylinder, four-horsepower motor shook the frame, which was mounted on four bicycle wheels. A bicycle saddle provided a seat on top of the three-gallon gas tank. A few weeks later, Ford added a buggy seat to the vehicle and drove the nine miles to the old homestead in Dearborn with his wife and son Edsel.

Ford later recalled that Clara gave him steadfast encouragement throughout those years of struggle. "My wife believed in me so much that when many were doubting my early experiments, I called her 'The Believer.'"

By now, Ford was working as chief engineer for the Detroit Edison Co. at eighteen hundred dollars a year, a high salary in the late 1890s. Meanwhile, he sold that first car for two hundred dollars and used the money to design and build an even better car.

Ford's work had attracted the attention of several businessmen who in 1898, when he was thirty-five, offered Ford ten thousand dollars—enough to pay for the manufacture of ten cars. In 1899, Ford left his job to become chief engineer of the newly organized Detroit Automobile Co.

But the arrangement was short-lived, and he and his backers split up. (The reorganized company eventually became the Cadillac Motor Car Company.)

With another group of investors, Ford became chief engineer of the Henry Ford Company in 1901. But again, disagreement arose between Ford and the other stockholders, so the company was dissolved in 1902 when he was thirty-nine years old. In both cases the disputes were caused by Ford's refusal to be hurried in his experiments. He insisted that to be successful, the company must manufacture a car that could be sold at a low price. He also demanded that profits be plowed back into the company to build business. The investors balked at Ford's policies. Rather than give up his beliefs, he left.

"Life is a series of experiences, each one of which makes us bigger, even though sometimes it's hard to realize it," he once said.

Nearly forty, and still falling far short of his dream of becoming an auto manufacturer, Ford continued to work on his engines, refining and improving them. He found a way to overcome each setback. "I have always refused to recognize that there are impossibilities," Ford said years later.

Success after Forty

Ford went back to his experimenting in another little shop of his own, working on a four-cylinder motor. Intent on getting speed—a mile a minute—he and others then began building racing cars which drew tremendous publicity because of their exploits on the track. Ford built two models—the "Arrow" and "999." After racing them, Ford said, "Going over Niagara Falls would have been but a pastime after a ride in one of them."

Meanwhile, thousands of automobiles were being manufactured by companies such as Oldsmobile. Ford knew he could build the best car for the money. He went in search of backers who believed in him—and his ideas.

Just days before his fortieth birthday, in 1903, Ford found ten more investors and he launched the Ford Motor Company. The new firm was soon at work producing the Fordmobile, to sell for $850. This was the Model A, constructed for practical, everyday purposes. Utility, not comfort, was Ford's aim.

"The business went along almost as if by magic," he once said. "The cars gained a reputation for standing up. They were tough, they were simple, and they were well made."

Pursuers Of Visions

In 1908, he introduced the Model T. Within five years, a half-million of the unattractive but efficient Model Ts were on the road. "Any customer can have a car painted any color that he wants, so long as it is black," Ford said.

By 1911, only eight years after he founded the company, over four thousand Ford employees were producing 34,500 cars in the newly built plant. Increased demand called for greatly increased speed in production. That's when Ford came up with one of his greatest brainstorms—the assembly line. With the moving assembly belt in 1913, more cars per day were driving off under their own power.

When critics complained that the repetitious work on the assembly line would cause boredom and unhappiness to the employees, Ford offered a quick solution. The Ford Company made the sensational announcement in 1914 that all its workers would receive a minimum wage of five dollars for an eight-hour day. The news rocked the work world—and Ford became the most famous man in the country.

In 1919, when he was fifty-five years old, Ford bought up all the stock not owned by his family. The company, which now had a capitalization of one hundred million dollars, was a family property. And it was fast becoming one of the country's biggest manufacturers of all time.

Ford's early vision of the future of transportation had brought him much satisfaction—and money. But he said the money alone didn't bring him a peace of mind.

"If money is your hope for independence, you will never have [security]," he said. "The only real security that a man can have in this world is a reserve of knowledge, experience, and ability."

CHASERS OF DREAMS

If one advances confidently in the direction of his dreams,
and endeavors to live the life which he has imagined,
he will meet a success unexpected in common hours.

— Henry David Thoreau

George Foreman

George Foreman refused to let others tell him he couldn't make a comeback. He had a dream to catch—and, by God, he was going to catch it.

Growing up in a poverty-stricken environment, Foreman turned pro in 1969 at the age of twenty. Merciless in the ring, he KOed thirty-three opponents, setting the stage for his first shot at the

> *"God bless all the people who know that being forty is not a death sentence."*

heavyweight crown when he faced Smokin' Joe Frazier in 1973. Foreman claimed the title after flooring Frazier six times before the fight was ended in the second round.

Foreman went on to defend his title twice. But then he felt the sting of defeat in 1974 when Muhammad Ali knocked him out. Losing that fight "knocked me off my axis," Foreman recalled. "The heavyweight title meant much more to me after I lost it then when I held it. Without it, I was nothing."

Some fire had gone out of Foreman's heart. He continued to fight but after dropping a twelve-round decision to Jimmy Young in 1977, Foreman gave up boxing. He was twenty-eight years old.

A year later, George started a new life as an ordained minister and established his own Church of the Lord Jesus Christ near Houston. He also founded the George Foreman Youth and Community Center, created to give troubled youngsters an alternative to delinquency. He had bought a warehouse and refurbished it, complete with a basketball court and a boxing ring. He also fitted the center with weights, boxing gloves, and other sports equipment. "The center was a haven for these kids, safe from the outside world," he said.

Chasers of Dreams

Foreman paid for the upkeep of the center out of his own pocket. But the expenses were eating into his savings a little more each month. Finally in 1987, when Foreman was thirty-eight, his attorney told him, "George, it's great that you're trying to help people. But I have to tell you, you're going to be the saddest boxing story since Joe Louis began standing out there at Caesars Palace shaking hands. You can't afford to keep this place up. You're going to have to pull back."

Recalled George, "I felt like crying, not just because what he said was true, but because I didn't want anybody, even him, to know what I already knew." Foreman faced financial ruin if he continued to fund the center; yet if he closed the place, he would let the kids down. "These kids were jumping on buses every day to come to my center. If I didn't take care of them, who would? They didn't need to hear about my financial problems."

Foreman at first attempted to raise extra money by accepting honorariums for speaking engagements, but he felt embarrassed when, at one gathering, they passed around the plate for donations. There had to be another way. Recalled George, "And then the thought struck me: *I know how to get money. I'm going to be heavyweight champ of the world. Again.*"

Success after Forty

He was a thirty-eight-year-old, 315-pound minister who hadn't boxed professionally in ten years. Those who knew him best gave him a chance—a very slim one—of seeing his dream come true. No one else did. But that didn't matter to Foreman. He believed in himself.

After getting the guarded blessings of his family, George submitted to two days of medical tests. Although he was terribly overweight, the doctors pronounced him healthy. Unfortunately, his old boxing trunks didn't fit. Neither did the rest of his boxing gear. But he wasn't concerned. He had a dream to catch.

His wife Joan acted as his first trainer. She would drive him as far as ten miles away from home, drop him off and then wait for him to jog back home. "Before, even as champ, I'd never run longer than three miles," Foreman recalled. "Now at age thirty-eight, I was running mini-marathons. In fact, for the first time, I discovered what athletes meant when they talked about getting their 'second wind.' Forcing myself through the leg-dragging phase, I'd suddenly be refreshed, able to go as far as my willpower allowed, and that seemed like infinity."

Foreman trained harder than ever. "A returning fighter pushing forty can't be ordinary," he said. "He has to be extraordinary. He can't be in good shape; he has to be in exceptional shape. Since it was the legs that would betray my age, the legs had to believe they were twenty years younger."

George tried to concoct a business deal with investors. In exchange for up-front cash to pay for the five-hundred-thousand-dollar training expenses, he offered them 40 percent of all future boxing earnings. But no one would advance him the money. Who wanted to back an over-weight, middle-aged preacher who hadn't boxed in ten years? Undeterred, Foreman was forced to spend the money he had set aside for his retirement. But to George it was worth the risk—because he knew, *he just knew*, that his dream would come true.

Finally, after whittling down to a fighting weight of 267 pounds, George felt he was ready to stage his dramatic comeback in California. But he had to hurdle an unexpected obstacle. The athletic commission at first refused to license him because of his age, even though he had passed its physical.

At a hearing, the commission's doctor feared that at Foreman's age, he could get seriously hurt in the ring. The commission asked George why he wanted to fight. "Life, liberty, and the pursuit of happiness," he replied simply.

Success after Forty

A lawyer for the state then told the commission, "The man has satisfied all your requirements. So if there's nothing wrong with him, you should give him a license." The commission reluctantly agreed.

When George publicly announced his return to the ring, sportswriters scoffed at the idea. "I didn't mind," recalled Foreman. "They could be excused for their ignorance. How were they to know what was in my heart, soul, and mind?"

When George entered the ring for his first postretirement fight against Steve Zouski, the crowd gave him a standing ovation. During the bout, the thirty-eight-year-old ex-champ displayed some of his long-lost punching power and won by a technical knockout. Buoyed by his success, Foreman went on to defeat twenty-three more opponents over the next three years. But the experts weren't too impressed because only one of his opponents—Gerry Cooney—was a ranked contender.

But Foreman knew what he was doing. He deliberately chose to take a longer path to his dream. "I'd seen others like Muhammad Ali and Joe Frazier fail in their comebacks because they were looking for overnight success," he said. "I treated myself like a younger man, a prospect."

Chasers of Dreams

Most sportswriters, who didn't understand his long-term strategy, kept taking jabs at George. His opponents, said one writer, "could scarcely have been less dangerous if pulled from a mortuary drawer." Another scribe claimed Foreman's punches could have been timed with a sundial.

To his credit, George took the snide remarks with good humor and beat the writers at their own game, counterpunching with an appealing combination of self-deprecating humor. Among his favorite lines: "People say I won't fight anybody who is not on a respirator. That's a lie. They have to be off the respirator for at least a week." "Dieting interferes with my sense of contentment, which is worse than being heavy." And to prove it, he would devour several cheeseburgers in front of the journalists.

By the age of forty-one, George had become a folk hero to the over-forty set. Said one writer, "Foreman has captured the imagination of the multitude who dream of seeing a middle-aged fat man make nonsense of natural laws of physical decline."

After putting up with the rigorous training, the scoffing nonbelievers, and the bruising bouts, Foreman at last found himself one step away from attaining his dream. The forty-two-year-old Foreman would face heavyweight champion Evander Holyfield, a twenty-eight-year-old boxer at the peak of his career.

No one expected George to win. Most didn't think he even could go the distance. But Foreman fought with skill and moxie and threw several punches that hurt the champion. It wasn't enough. To Foreman's great disappointment, the three judges scored a unanimous—but close—decision for Holyfield. George had missed his golden opportunity to win the title. His only consolation was that he had surprised the experts with his stunning performance.

"We didn't retreat and we kept our dignity," he told the press. "So everyone at home can take pride that, while we may not win all the points, we made a point. Everyone grab your Geritol, and let's toast. Hip-hip-hooray!"

Despite the defeat, George continued his quest for that elusive second title. But his fortunes looked bleak in 1993 when Foreman, who was now forty-four, lost a twelve-round decision to Tommy Morrison. Sportswriters urged him to quit. And for a while it looked like he would. He accepted an offer to star in a network sitcom called *George*, about a former boxer working with kids. But the series was canceled after eight episodes.

It was just as well. Foreman had strayed from the path toward his goal. After a little soul-searching, George realized that his dream of becoming a champion remained as strong as ever. He still had the drive to excel, to do whatever was necessary to become champion once again.

Despite the odds, Foreman managed to set up a title bout in 1994. He knew it would be his one last attempt to catch his dream. The forty-five-year-old Foreman would face a champion who was young enough to be his son—World Boxing Association and International Boxing Federation title-holder Michael Moorer, who had dethroned Holyfield.

Once again, Foreman had to fight in the courtroom before he could fight in the ring. Initially the WBA refused to sanction the match, citing Foreman's advanced age and his fourteen-month layoff.

Foreman went to court and testified, "I've wanted to be heavyweight champ of the world ever since I reentered the ring in 1987. It means more to me probably than anything else athletically in the world. I wanted to fight for the title to show the world not only that I can win this thing, but that age forty is truly not a deficit."

After hearing hours of testimony from other witnesses, Judge Donald

Mosley gave his decision: "It might well be argued that Mr. Foreman, if he can sit and listen to eleven hours of lawyers, would have no problem going ten rounds with anyone."

In November 1994 in Las Vegas, Foreman stepped into the ring, knowing this was his last chance. Fans leaped to their feet, chanting "George! George! George!" Recalled Foreman, "A lot of those people, including some of those cheering loudest, probably believed in their hearts that what the 'experts' said was true: George is too old, too fat, and too slow to have any real chance of winning the championship. For them, I was a symbol, the man who refused to accept middle age."

The underdog Foreman, wearing the same trunks he had donned twenty years earlier in his fight with Ali, fought the way he had orchestrated his comeback—patiently. Moorer dominated round after round while the crafty Foreman waited for the opportunity to land his knockout punch—the hard right.

As they entered the final round, Moorer was ahead on points. But the young champ looked tired. Foreman still had spring in his legs. As the bell sounded to begin the last round, Foreman knew it was now or never.

Chasers of Dreams

If he wanted to become champion again, George couldn't just win the round on points; he had to knock out his opponent.

With every punch and jab, Foreman unleashed a furious assault honed by years of hard work and high hopes. A left hook to the ear . . . then three more in the same spot. . . . A left jab . . . a strong right to the forehead. Moorer was reeling now. Foreman then moved in and drove a jack-hammer right that drilled into the champ's chin, sending him crashing to the mat.

Seconds later, the referee counted Moorer out—and the arena erupted in bedlam. Everybody was jumping up and down, hugging strangers, cheering themselves hoarse. "I never saw so many obviously happy people in one place," George recalled. "It was a joyful noise they made. The victory belonged to them. That was something you could feel. For a moment, they were free. Something I'd done had given them free-dom. I hope I never do anything to unfreeze that moment in time for anyone who watched and felt that way."

George Foreman had done the impossible. He caught his dream of recapturing the title as heavyweight champion of the world—and he did it just two months shy of his forty-sixth birthday.

Mary Kay Ash

Mary Kay Ash founded one of the first and most successful woman-owned nationwide businesses in the country because she acted on her dreams—and was willing to work hard to make them come true.

Born in Texas in 1915, Mary Kay learned responsibility at an early age, having to care for her ailing father while her mother worked to support the family. Her mother repeatedly told her, "Anything anyone else can do, you can do better." And Mary Kay believed her.

Mary Kay discovered that she could sell—and liked it. She married shortly after graduating from high school and, while raising a family, sold sets of books called the *Child Psychology Bookshelf.*

> **"Y**ou can be as successful as you want to be—if you are willing to pay the price and have the courage to dream.**"**

Success after Forty

She and her husband soon worked as a team selling expensive pressure cookers and frying pans at get-togethers.

In 1939, at the age of twenty-four, Mary Kay got another job in direct sales as a representative for the Houston-based Stanley Home Products Company, which made such things as floor brushes and cleaning agents. At her first Stanley sales convention, the company rewarded the top saleswoman with an alligator-skin handbag. Mary Kay was so psyched-up she told the company's president, "I intend to be the top saleswoman next year." The president replied, "Somehow I think you will."

Recalled Mary Kay: "Those few words literally changed my life. The president of the company thought I could do it. After that, I could not let him down."

Mary Kay persuaded the top saleswoman to hold a demonstration party during the convention. While the woman gave her sales talk, Mary Kay transcribed her words in nineteen pages of notes. "That sales demonstration became my railroad track and those notes became my springboard to success."

The next year, Mary Kay achieved her goal. She was named the top saleswoman. But to her disappointment, she received a light for night fishing as her reward, not a fancy purse. "Bag or not," she recalled, "I had become queen of sales by setting a goal, breaking it down into small, realistic tasks, and broadcasting it to the world."

After World War II, Mary Kay suffered an emotional setback when her husband asked for a divorce, which she gave him. Now she had to support herself and her three children. "I had a very hard time accepting the divorce," she said. "For almost a year, I felt that I had failed as a woman, as a wife, and as a person."

To make matters worse, she developed symptoms of rheumatoid arthritis. Doctors warned she could become totally incapacitated. Rather than give up, she worked that much harder as a Stanley saleswoman.

"The competitive spirit my mother had instilled in me kept me going through some very difficult days," she recalled. "I competed with myself. On Saturday, I wanted my earnings for the week to be a little more than the week before. When I was successful, it wasn't because I was any more talented than the next salesperson; I was just willing to make more sacrifices. I was willing to work hard, and pay the price for success."

Success after Forty

She gave up more sleep so she could do her housework and care for her children. And she gave up a social life. Her income increased—and, incredibly, her symptoms disappeared.

In 1952, at the age of thirty-seven, Mary Kay resigned from Stanley and began work as the national training director for the World Gift Company, a Dallas-based direct sales firm. It was there that she fell victim to blatant sexism. Time and again she would make a presentation to the otherwise all-male hierarchy. And time and again she was ignored.

Recalled Mary Kay, "Every time I made a suggestion—remember, now, we were working with an all-women [sales force]—and every time I suggested something they [the directors] would say, 'Mary Kay, you're thinking like a woman again.' I would think about how something they were going to do would affect the women. Not how it would affect the company, but how those women out there would react and feel about what they [the directors] were going to do. I would interpret that for them [the directors], and they would say, 'Look, we've got to worry about the bottom line.'"

Worst of all, she would train men, only to see them leapfrog over her in the corporate ladder. In 1963, after a man whom she had trained was named her supervisor and given a salary twice as high as hers, Mary Kay quit. She was forty-eight years old and in the third year of her second marriage.

After she left, Mary Kay began to write down her ideas for a career guide that might help women avoid some of the pitfalls she had encountered as a woman in the business world. She embarked on the project to rid herself of the anger she felt over the mistreatment she had experienced and over the opportunities that had been closed to her because of her sex. She also harbored resentments about company rules and procedures that completely disregarded workers' personal concerns.

So Mary Kay began to dream of a different kind of company—one that would offer women unlimited potential in terms of both income and flexible hours. "I envisioned a company in which any woman could become just as successful as she wanted to be. The doors would be open wide to opportunity.

"I asked myself, 'Why are you theorizing about a dream company? Why don't you just start one?'"

Setting aside her writing project, she thought about what product she might sell. It had to be something that women could believe in, could use and recommend with all their heart. "And in direct sales, it's very important to have a product that will be used up, so there are several sales to be made." She decided to market skin-care products. Back then, cosmetic companies were just selling makeup, not teaching skin care. Mary Kay thought it would be better if a salesperson went into the home of a woman who had invited four or five friends for a demonstration. That way, the salesperson could teach skin care and help each customer determine what cosmetics were best for her.

The more Mary Kay thought about her dream company, the more excited she became. She thought back to her childhood and the heavy load of responsibility she had to bear. She thought of her mother. "Mother constantly reinforced my self-image that I could do anything in this world I wanted to do if I wanted to do it badly enough and I was willing to pay the price."

With part of her life savings of five thousand dollars, Mary Kay obtained the rights to the formulas for the homemade skin-care creams and lotions that she had been using for years. The creams were prepared and bottled by a woman who had scented and reformulated various substances that her father had used in tanning leather. The creams had kept his hands remarkably soft throughout his working life.

Mary Kay then used the balance of her savings to buy the requisite chemical substances and containers, a few furnishings, and some used office equipment. She leased a five-hundred-square-foot storefront in a large office building complex in Dallas. She also hired a chemical manufacturer to produce her basic skin-care set, which consisted of only five products. While her husband planned to deal with the legal and financial matters for the company, Mary Kay recruited a sales force of nine of her friends.

Then tragedy struck. One month before the scheduled opening of the company—called Beauty by Mary Kay—her husband Mel died of a heart attack. While the grief-stricken widow made funeral arrangements, her attorney and accountant advised her to take a financial loss and give up the idea of starting her own business or face potentially bigger losses. Her lawyer even showed her a pamphlet about the large number of cosmetics companies that failed each year.

Success after Forty

But Mary Kay had a dream that she refused to give up. Her children encouraged her to proceed. Her twenty-year-old son Richard even quit his job and became her partner (at half the salary he was making before). Since her savings were committed to the venture and her dream remained as vivid as ever, Mary Kay marched forward with her plans.

With its entire inventory of skin-care sets and a few cosmetics displayed on inexpensive Sears shelving, Beauty by Mary Kay opened its doors on September 13, 1963, with the forty-eight-year-old widow brimming with confidence.

In the storefront as well as in people's homes, her nine saleswomen, whom Mary Kay called "consultants," gave facials and showed off the company's products. Instructed by Mary Kay never to use high-pressure salesmanship, the consultants held classes where they taught women how to use the products. "Your role is not to sell cosmetics," Mary Kay told the consultants. "Your role is to ask yourself, 'What can I do to send these women home feeling more beautiful on the inside as a result?'"

Within four months, sales of Mary Kay products totaled thirty-four thousand dollars. She and her son soon had to rent a second space in which to store sufficient inventory to meet demand and supply their rapidly growing sales crew. After eight months her older son came to Dallas to manage the warehouse and to assist his mother and brother with filling and packing orders.

"Our hard work paid off," recalled Mary Kay, who was working sixteen to eighteen hours a day. "The first calendar year brought us $198,000 in wholesale sales, and at the end of the second year, we had reached the unbelievable total of eight hundred thousand dollars."

Mary Kay Cosmetics, as the firm was now called, saw the sales force grow to three thousand consultants. The company moved into a bigger building to accommodate offices and a five-thousand-square-foot warehouse. In 1968, five years after going into business for herself, Mary Kay became a millionaire when her company went public.

Today, the corporate headquarters are housed in a nine-building complex in Dallas. Her sales force, which started with nine women, numbered over 325,000 consultants by 1995—the year when earnings topped over one billion dollars. Mary Kay's personal worth has been estimated at $320 million.

Success after Forty

According to the company's literature, 80 percent of the 3 percent of American women who earn more than $100,000 annually are associated with Mary Kay. The average annual income of the more than ninety Mary Kay national sales directors is well into six figures. Hundreds of the seven thousand Mary Kay directors earn more than fifty thousand dollars a year and many others earn more than one hundred thousand dollars. "It is estimated that more women have earned over one million dollars from their Mary Kay careers than at any other company in the world," says the company.

Not bad for what once was a storefront business started by a forty-eight-year-old widow who had never run a company.

Ian Fleming

Ian Fleming almost waited too long to make his dream come true. Not until he fell into a deep career rut did he finally pursue his dream with a vigor he hadn't felt since he was a college graduate.

In 1929, at the age of twenty-one, the English-born Fleming began a career in journalism as Moscow correspondent for the Reuters news agency. He stayed with the agency for four years, learned Russian, and enjoyed himself immensely, although he didn't earn much money.

He started a new career in finance but left it in 1939 when he began serving during World War II as personal assistant to

> *"After the age of forty, time begins to be important and one is inclined to say 'yes' to every experience. One should, of course, be taught to say 'yes' from childhood, but wet feet, catching cold, getting a temperature, and breaking something add to a permanent 'no' that is apt to become a permanent ball and chain."*

the director of British Naval Intelligence. He made a name for himself by showing a total lack of awe for the admirals, generals, and air marshals around him. "There are only two people you should ever call 'sir,'" he once told a friend, "God and the King."

Because of his position, Fleming soon knew more secrets and had more real power than most of the senior officers, and he swiftly climbed in rank to commander. Although an outsider to the special operations carried out by British spies, Fleming was an observer to their plots and schemes.

Occasionally Fleming went on a foreign assignment that held minimal risks. On such missions he carried a commando fighting knife and a fountain pen that ejected a cloud of tear gas when the clip was pressed. He once took command of a group of Royal Marines that accompanied attack troops to seize enemy codes and equipment.

Another time, while in a casino at Estoril, Portugal, Fleming recognized German agents playing the card game *chemin de fer*. He joined their table, planning to beat them at their game, take all their funds, and thus squash any of their nefarious plans. Fleming left the game penniless.

Chasers of Dreams

When the war ended, the thirty-seven-year-old ex-officer became the foreign editor of the *London Sunday Times*. During bleak winter days, he fantasized about moving to Jamaica and writing novels. Fleming dreamed of romanticizing his own life in the service into a character who was an elegant, amorous, and indestructible agent of Her Majesty's Secret Service.

In 1946, he fulfilled part of his dream when he built a vacation house in Jamaica that he called Goldeneye. "I was determined that one day Goldeneye would be better known than any of the great houses that had been there so long and achieved nothing," he once said.

Meanwhile, the day-to-day grind of his job in London was getting to him. Foreign politics bored him. He seldom traveled and never wrote an editorial or a foreign news report. He was now forty-two and felt he had no future in the newspaper business. He kept dreaming of becoming a novelist.

Still, he wasn't motivated enough to make the commitment of time and energy. However, in 1950, he read the potboiler *My Gun Is Quick* by Mickey Spillane, which he didn't like. Fleming thought he could write a much better novel. The mental picture of his spy character began coming into much clearer focus.

Success after Forty

James Bond was born in January 1952 at Goldeneye. At the time, Fleming was forty-three and convinced that his newspaper career had bottomed out. Figuring it was now or never, Fleming sat down in front of his twenty-year-old Imperial portable typewriter and brought his alter-ego to life. Fleming had no notes; just memories of his days in naval intelligence and the plots he had been conjuring up in his mind over the years during those long gray days at work.

It was time to live his fantasy by writing it down.

He named his hero James Bond after the author of the book *Birds of the West Indies*, which was laying on a nearby table. "I wanted the simplest, dullest, plainest-sounding name I could find," Fleming recalled. "James Bond seemed perfect."

Fleming wrote about two thousand words a day for seven straight weeks. He called his novel *Casino Royale*. Its high point was a tense baccarat game between Bond and a Communist agent called Le Chiffre. The game—obviously compensating for Fleming's own defeat at Estoril—ended with the Communist's financial and political ruin.

Fleming sent the manuscript to a publisher he knew who loved it but demanded several revisions. Knowing his days were numbered at work, Fleming bought a symbol to remind himself where his future lay—a gold Royal typewriter that cost him $174. In a note to his publisher about the new Royal, Fleming said, "As you see, I am treating my muse with small respect and largely as a means to move from one scaly profession to another."

He was working harder than ever now to make his dream of being a best-selling author come true. He believed in himself so much that he wrote a second novel, *To Live and Let Die*, before his debut book had even been published.

To Fleming's great disappointment, *Casino Royale* was only a modest success in England, initially selling about eight thousand copies. In the United States, Doubleday, Norton, and Knopf all turned down the chance to publish it. Macmillan published the book, which sold a mere four thousand copies in its first year in the United States.

But Fleming was now living his dream and he wasn't going to give it up. Married with one son, Fleming divided his time between London and his house in Jamaica, where he spent four months each year typing out his annual Bond thriller. He wrote about the exploits of Agent 007 in *Moonraker, From Russia with Love,* and *Dr. No.* But sales of his books didn't take off until the first of the Bond films, Dr. No, introduced the agent to a huge new audience in 1961.

Within two years of the movie, sales in hardcover and softcover of Fleming's books soared to over seventeen million. By the time of his death in 1964 at the age of fifty-six, his Bond books had sold over forty million copies worldwide.

While writing one of his last books, *You Only Live Twice,* Fleming said, "I think it's an absolute miracle that an elderly person like me can go on turning out these books with such zest. It's really a terrible indictment of my own character—they're so adolescent. But they're fun. I think people like them because they are fun."

As for seeing his dream come true, he said, "Everyone must try. Those who succeed through their own endeavors are heroes."

K.T. Oslin

K.T. Oslin labored in obscurity and near-poverty for years before she discovered what she really wanted to do with her life—become a country music star. But after a few false starts, K.T. was on the verge of calling it quits in 1987, fearing her dream was unattainable.

After all, she was a forty-five-year-old unknown trying to crack the big-time at an age when many recording careers are sliding downhill. But her dream would not fade. By the end of the year, she was living out her dream—as a rising country music star whose debut album had gone platinum.

Today, the down-home diva has found a legion of fans who love her music as much as her inspiring life story.

> **"I** let people know that forty isn't the age to pack it in."

Success after Forty

K.T. (short for Kay Toinette) didn't have a stable childhood. Her father died when she was only five years old. She and her brother were uprooted repeatedly as her mother, a hospital lab technician, married and divorced four times.

While growing up in Houston, Oslin learned to play the piano and got involved in the theater. In 1967, at the age of twenty-five, K.T. moved to New York, hoping to make her mark on the stage. But after a couple of chorus jobs, she knew musical theater wasn't for her. "I didn't have the devotion to the theater that people must have in order to succeed."

So K.T. bounced between acting in commercials and singing jingles. "Singing should be a really joyous thing, but it isn't when you're babbling about dishes or soap," she said. "In my typical TV commercial roles, I was usually a midwestern housewife wearing a plaid shirt. I hated looking like that.

"I eked out a living—just enough that I didn't have to go and be a waitress or a sign painter or something."

Making TV commercials, like the one in which she was a happy housewife talking about her husband's hemorrhoids, may have paid the bills, but it didn't satisfy Oslin's creative longings. So she turned to what she loved most—music.

Her inspiration to write songs began in 1978 when she was thirty-six. While on a trip, she stopped in a café in Due West, South Carolina. In the bathroom wall, she spotted graffiti that read, "I ain't never gonna love nobody but Cornell Crawford." K.T. decided to create a song based on that scrawled statement. Then she wrote more songs, almost all from a woman's point of view.

"When I started writing, to my total amazement, what came out was country even though I hadn't planned on it. I had never been much of a country fan except as a very young kid. But now I was writing to express stuff that I believed in all the way through."

Writing country tunes felt right to her. That's when she knew she wanted to be a country music star. So K.T. methodically went about honing her craft, working first with collaborators and then by herself. She gained confidence after penning a couple of songs that were recorded by country stars Gail Davies and Dottie West.

But Oslin's dream was far from realized. She still needed those commercial gigs to survive. For one job, she sang a country-style ad for Coke. "I was the Coca-Cola cowgirl, and I was sure it was going to be big," she recalled. "I was ready to buy a boat. Then I got a check for $38." The campaign bit the dust.

"I was so discouraged," said Oslin. "I thought, 'Oh, my God, I'm gonna die, and the only thing I'll be remembered for is a hemorrhoid commercial.'"

But she still had her dream. With a growing catalog of original songs, K.T. lit out for stardom. She put together a band with friends from Oklahoma to showcase her singing and songwriting talents. They did one show at a Manhattan club—and ended up eighty dollars in the hole after expenses.

Recalled K.T., "I asked my mother, 'Do you think I'm crazy for still being in this?' I was close to forty. And she turned to me and said, 'Well, I . . . yes.'"

Oslin kept plugging away and eventually landed a deal with Elektra Records in 1980 at the age of thirty-eight. Among the songs she brought to her Nashville recording sessions were "'80s Ladies" and "Younger Men." The former song was rejected by the label as "too women's lib." The latter song, about a sexually peaking woman of forty seeking a more youthful partner, was released. Unfortunately, it didn't fare well.

"Radio people practically slapped me on the wrist," K.T. said. "'We can't play this song,' they'd say, 'because it might offend our male listeners.' The problem was that men wrote most of the country music— middle-aged men singing about cheating on their wives and drinking."

The record company failed to pick up Oslin's option, leaving her crushed. "At first when they fire you, you go, 'Oh, my Lord, I've been fired.' And then you go, 'Well, of course I was fired. I don't really have any talent. They didn't fire Madonna, did they?' I was like a deflated thing that had lost all of its air."

After losing her contract, K.T. was ready to give up. "I got real fat and real depressed," she confessed. She hibernated in her bathrobe for a year, "sitting in the back of the cave licking my wounds." But in desperate need of income, she went back to commercials.

In 1985, at the age of forty-three, Oslin did a denture cream commercial in which she portrayed a screaming woman on a roller coaster. The job earned her ten thousand dollars, but it wasn't easy. It took forty-four takes. "I threw up in the bushes after the twelfth ride," she recalled. "I didn't feel good, but I managed to finish."

Feeling down about her current work status, Oslin still held onto her dream. She decided to give it one last shot. "I thought I had to do this or I'd wind up a clerk at Macy's or I'd be babbling in a padded room somewhere."

Her chances of success didn't look good. "I was overweight," she admitted. "I was forty-three and not a raving beauty, nor a funny, weird caricature, either. I didn't fit the mold on anything."

Oslin figured she would need seven thousand dollars to stage a one-night showcase in Nashville. She called her Aunt Reba, a successful stockbroker in Texas, and asked if she knew of any investor crazy enough to lend K.T. the money needed to rehearse a band and produce the show. Her aunt said sure—and then wrote out a check to K.T.

The audience raved about Oslin's performance, but the phone didn't ring the next day. Recalled K.T., "People would ask, 'How old is she? Thirty-five?' When they heard I was forty-five, they'd say, 'Too old.' I was devastated. Tell me I'm bad or that I can't write. Don't go telling me I'm too old."

Chasers of Dreams

But Harold Shedd, then producer of the country group Alabama, saw Oslin's showcase and was impressed. He arranged for RCA Records to hear tapes of her songs. When he called her back to report that RCA was enthusiastic, Oslin asked him what their reaction was to her age. "I said you were pushing forty," replied Shedd. "I just didn't tell them from which side."

In 1987 Oslin signed a recording contract, and three months later, her first RCA single came out, "'80s Ladies"—the one Elektra had rejected. RCA then produced her first album, *'80s Ladies*, in which eight of the nine songs were either written or cowritten by the self-taught composer. The songs are about women who've been around the block a few times. They're vulnerable yet they have inner strengths.

'80s Ladies leaped onto *Billboard's* country album chart at No. 15, becoming the highest-placing solo debut album by a woman in country music history. Critics hailed *'80s Ladies* as a wryly funny, tuneful blend of the cynical and romantic. The album, which became a certified platinum, especially struck a chord with female baby boomers.

After twenty years in the entertainment minor leagues, K.T. had burst onto the country music scene at an age when many other careers begin to dim. In just two months, she had gone from obscurity to a *Tonight Show* guest. Her career took off. Oslin's second album, *This Woman,* was voted best of the year by the Academy of Country Music and was certified platinum. The winner of three Grammy Awards, Oslin was the Country Music Association's top female vocalist of 1988. Her third album, *Love in a Small Town,* was certified gold.

"I'm a hardheaded, stubborn thing," K.T. declared. "It took me a lot of time with little money to fulfill my dream. I had to bash and get bashed, but in the end it came out all right."

However, grueling tours to promote her albums took a near-fatal toll on her. In 1995, Oslin underwent an emergency heart operation—a triple-bypass—and afterward decided to slow down. She continues to write songs, but has given up performing on the road. "I was close to buying the farm, and now I want to have fun on the farm."

When asked after her first album if she regretted all the years she spent in obscurity, K.T. replied, "I'd rather be starting now than ending now."

— EMBRACERS OF OPPORTUNITY —

We are told that talent creates its own opportunities. But it sometimes seems that intense desire creates not only its own opportunities but its own talents.

— Eric Hoffer

Ray Kroc

Throughout his childhood in Chicago, Ray Kroc was looking for ways to better his life.

"When I was a kid, I saw my dad struggling to make ends meet on a meager salary," Kroc once said. "I resolved then to make money. I knew the only way to do that was to find the right opportunity."

> "**You** must take advantage of any opportunity that comes along—and I have always done that."

Success after Forty

A high school dropout, Kroc wandered into the entertainment business as a jazz pianist. When he married at the age of twenty, he left the music scene to work as a salesman for the Lily-Tulip Cup Company. Not long after that he became musical director for a pioneer radio station, WGES, in Chicago, playing the piano, arranging the music, accompanying singers, and hiring musicians. (One of his discoveries was a song-and-comedy team named Sam and Henry, who later became famous as Amos 'n' Andy.)

After about a year and a half of radio work, Kroc left WGES because of a new opportunity to sell real estate in Florida, which was in the midst of the great land boom of the 1920s. He worked for a company that peddled swampy property in Fort Lauderdale. When the boom collapsed late in 1926, Kroc was flat broke. He played piano in a nightclub to earn enough money to send his wife and daughter back to Chicago by train.

Later, he drove back in a Model T Ford. "I will never forget that drive as long as I live," he recalled. "I was stone broke. I didn't have an overcoat, a topcoat, or a pair of gloves. I drove into Chicago on icy streets. When I got home, I was frozen stiff, disillusioned, and broke."

But he had a dream that one day, he would make it big. He didn't know how or where or when it would happen. He just knew it would. All he had to do was find the right opportunity.

Kroc returned to his old job as a salesman for Lily-Tulip and was soon made its midwestern sales manager. In 1937, at the age of thirty-five, he came upon a new invention called the Prince Castle Multimixer—a machine that could mix five milk shakes at once. This, he told himself, was *the* opportunity. And he grabbed it.

After seventeen years of selling paper cups for Lily-Tulip and climbing to the top of the organization's sales ladder, he felt ready to be his own boss. He quit his job again, made a deal with the inventor, and soon became the world's exclusive agent for the Multimixer.

"It wasn't easy to give up security and a well-paying job to strike out on my own," Kroc recalled. "My wife was shocked and incredulous.

"'You are risking your whole future if you do this, Ray,' she said. 'You are thirty-five years old, and you are going to start all over again as if you were twenty? This Multimixer seems good now, but what if it turns out to be just a fad and fails?'

"'You just have to trust my instincts,' I said. 'I am positive this is going to be a winner.'"

Over the next twenty years, Kroc traveled to thousands of drugstore soda fountains and dairy bars in the nation, pushing his product. He earned a fair living, but it wasn't the winner he thought it would be.

"It was a rewarding struggle," Kroc said in his biography. "I loved it. Yet I was alert to other opportunities. I have a saying that goes, 'As long as you're green, you're growing. As soon as you're ripe you start to rot.' And I was as green as a Shamrock Shake on St. Patrick's Day when I heard about an incredible thing that was happening with my Multimixer out in California."

In 1954, the fifty-two-year-old salesman visited a hamburger stand in San Bernardino, California, which was operating eight of his Multimixers—more than any other restaurant. Kroc discovered that the owners, brothers Maurice and Richard McDonald, were doing a remarkable business selling only hamburgers, french fries, and milk shakes. Everything was prepared in advance; everything was uniform.

Kroc was amazed at the crowds that waited in line at the stand. He was impressed with the restaurant's speed of service and its cleanliness. The McDonald brothers served a standard hamburger for fifteen cents, and the french fries were kept warm and crispy.

"I was fascinated by the simplicity and effectiveness of the system," Kroc recalled. "Each step in producing the limited menu was stripped down to its essence and accomplished with a minimum of effort.

"That night in my motel room, I did a lot of heavy thinking about what I'd seen during the day. Visions of McDonald's restaurants dotting crossroads all over the country paraded through my brain. In each store, of course, were eight Multimixers whirring away and paddling a steady flow of cash into my pockets."

The next day, Kroc suggested he and the McDonald brothers open a series of restaurants. He was hoping they would say yes so he could boost his Multimixer sales. But they turned him down because they were content with what they had. So then he offered to open the other places himself as long as he could sell each unit his Multimixers. They agreed.

In his royalty arrangement with the McDonald brothers, Kroc would start a chain of hamburger restaurants on their format and give them one-half of 1 percent of the gross receipts. In 1955, Kroc opened the first McDonald's unit in the Chicago suburb of Des Plaines. He was fifty-three years old.

By the end of the year, he had sold two more McDonald's franchises in California. Realizing that the real profits lay in hamburgers, he sold his Multimixer rights in order to raise capital to expand the McDonald's venture. By 1960, Kroc had sold two hundred franchises, providing him with a gross franchise income of about $700,000 a year. But he knew McDonald's could be so much greater.

He decided that all new franchisees would be tenants; the company would select the site, build the restaurant, provide the equipment, and rent the total package to an operator. McDonald's would receive the rental from the lease as well as the franchising fee. It was a great plan, but it required money.

He needed $1.5 million to make it work. Unfortunately, he had neither the money nor credit. His main source of income had dried up when he was forced to sell his mixer business for $100,000 to pay for a divorce. Now his personal assets, including his house, totaled only $90,000.

Embracers of Opportunity

Kroc got the money he required from several insurance companies. In 1961, he bought out the McDonald brothers, paying $2.7 million for the trademark, copyrights, formulas, the Golden Arches symbol, and the name. By 1965, the number of units had mushroomed to 938 with sales of $170 million. Seven years later, when he was seventy, Kroc's company had sold more than ten billion hamburgers and, for the first time, had sales of more than one billion dollars.

Kroc said he saw a market opportunity in catering to budget-conscious families on wheels who want quick service, clean surroundings, and good food.

By 1995, McDonald's had fifteen thousand restaurants worldwide and sales of more than twenty-three billion dollars.

"My years of experience in selling paper cups and Multimixers paid off, because I knew exactly what hands held the strings I wanted to pull to get the job done," he said. "People have marveled at the fact that I didn't start McDonald's until I was fifty-two years old, and then I became a success overnight. But I was just like a lot of show-business personalities who work away quietly at their craft for years, and then, suddenly, they get the right break and make it big. I was an overnight success all right, but thirty years is a long, long night.

"There's almost nothing you can't accomplish if you set your mind to it. You're not going to get it free. You have to take risks. I don't mean to be a daredevil; that's crazy. But you have to take risks, and in some cases, you must go for broke. If you believe in something, you've got to be in it to the ends of your toes. Taking reasonable risks is part of the challenge. It's the fun."

King Camp Gillette

All his life, King Camp Gillette was tinkering and thinking of ways to improve things. He was a patient man and believed that one day, he would hit on that one big idea which would help consumers and make him a rich man.

King—named after a family friend—grew up in Chicago in the mid-1800s while his father worked as a patent agent. King and his two brothers were encouraged to work with their hands, to figure out how things work and how they might be made to work better. When the Gillettes lost almost everything in the disastrous fire that ravaged Chicago in 1871, the family moved to New York, where King learned the wholesale hardware business.

"*Sometimes the best ideas are the simplest.*"

Success after Forty

By the age of twenty-one, he was a traveling hardware salesman. But he did more than just sell it. He tinkered with metal products and soon received several patents for bushings and valves and conduits for electrical cables. However, none of these inventions made Gillette much money. "They made money for others, but seldom for myself," he recalled, "for I was unfortunately situated not having much time and little money with which to promote my inventions or place them on the market." He had to work for a living, traveling from city to city peddling his various wares.

In 1891, at the age of thirty-six, Gillette, now married with a child, joined the Baltimore Seal Company as a sales representative who covered New York and New England. The company's major product was a rubber bottle-stopper that could be pulled off with a metal loop. It was widely used by brewers and soft-drink bottlers.

William Painter, the president of the company, was an inventor who developed an improved stopper consisting of a cork-lined tin cap that was crimped tightly over a bottle top. It did so well that Baltimore Seal changed its name to Crown Cork & Seal Company. Painter's invention was soon the standard throughout the bottling industry and made him a very wealthy man. In a single year, it brought the inventor more than $350,000 in royalties.

As kindred inventive spirits, Gillette and Painter struck up a close personal as well as business relationship, and their conversations frequently turned to the development of useful and novel products. One day, Painter offered a piece of advice to King that would eventually change his life: "King, you are always thinking and inventing something. Why don't you try to think of something like the Crown Cork. When used once, it's thrown away. The customer keeps coming back for more—and with every additional customer you get, you are building a foundation of profit."

"But how many things are there like corks, pins, and needles?" Gillette asked.

"I don't know," Painter said. "It is not probably that you ever will find anything that is like the Crown Cork, but it won't do any harm to think about it."

Gillette did think about it. Indeed, he confessed later, Painter's words became an obsession with him. He spent most every free minute conjuring up one idea after another, all of which he rejected moments after thinking of them. He made lists of everyday items that might be improved upon or turned into a throwaway item. But like so many great ideas, the one he searched for didn't come easy; but when it came, it was a lightning flash of inspiration.

One morning in 1895, the forty-year-old traveling salesman was about to shave. As it was for millions of other men at the time, shaving was no fun. After lathering his face to moisten the whiskers and make them softer, the user put a highly sharpened three-inch blade to his face and proceeded to scrape away at his bearded growth.

Recalled Gillette, "When I started to shave, I found my razor dull, and it was not only dull but it was beyond the point of successful stropping, and it needed honing, for which it must be taken to a barber or to a cutler. As I stood there with the razor in my hand, my eyes resting on it as lightly as a bird settling down on its nest, the Gillette [safety] razor was born. I saw it all in a moment, and in that same moment many unvoiced questions were asked and answered more with the rapidity of a dream than by the slow process of reasoning.

"The thought occurred to me that no radical improvements had been made in razors, especially in razor blades, for several centuries, and it flashed through my mind that if by any possibility razor blades could be constructed and made cheap enough to do away with honing and stropping and permit the user to replace dull blades by new ones, such improvements would be highly important in that art."

When faced with the necessity of honing an old-fashioned razor, he thought of using instead a thin blade of steel, sharpened at both edges, clamped between plates and held together by a handle. The wafer-thin steel would be so inexpensive that the shaver could merely discard it when it grew dull.

He tinkered with the idea for six years before forming a safety razor company with no offices, no factory, no full-time employees, and only the barest of money. He and his two partners all had other jobs.

Gillette's first model was a dismal disappointment. Back then, conventional wisdom said that the ideal razor blade should be expensive and last a lifetime with proper stropping, honing, and care. Now came King Gillette, a forty-six-year-old traveling salesman, who claimed that blades should be made of cheap sheet steal and thrown away after a couple of shaves.

Success after Forty

People who knew better—cutlers, metallurgists, and the like—told him that it couldn't be done. The kindest thing that could be said of Gillette's idea was that it was laughable. Years later, Gillette would concede that only blissful ignorance carried him through the tough times. "If I had been technically trained, I would have quit or probably never would have begun."

Before the company had sold a single blade, it was in debt by thousands of dollars. "We were backed up to the wall with our creditors lined up in front waiting for the signal to fire," said Gillette. But he had seen his idea come too far to let it die at the hands of bill collectors.

He went to businessman John Joyce, who years earlier had backed an ill-fated venture of Gillette's. Despite the fact that King owed Joyce $20,000 from that failure, the inventor boldly asked the millionaire to help prop up his shaky razor company. But first Gillette had given him one of the sample razors. Joyce was impressed enough to give him the capital he needed.

In 1903—when Gillette was forty-eight—the Gillette Safety Razor Company began selling its product. The first year the company sold a paltry fifty-one razors and 168 blades. But the important thing was that there were people out there willing to pay five dollars for a new kind of safety razor, and the backers who believed in the product were certain that these first few sales were harbingers of far greater things to come.

Although he was president of his company, Gillette still earned his living as a traveling salesman for Crown Cork & Seal, which now paid him $5,000 a year. The company gave him a raise and sent him to England even though he didn't want to go.

By the end of 1904, the number of sales had jumped to ninety thousand razors and 12.4 million blades. Through clever advertising and merchandising, the business steadily expanded until eight plants in various parts of the world were built to meet the demand. Today, the Gillette enterprise is a 6.7-billion-dollar business.

The middle-aged traveling salesman had followed through on an idea that forever changed the way men shaved. As Gillette conceded years later, his razor blade "doesn't appeal to the average mind as being a great invention." On the other hand, he added, nothing had "equalled the Gillette razor in its saving of time over the system it displaced."

Best of all, he added, it was a simple idea.

Jean Nidetch

When Jean Nidetch was an overweight housewife, she never dreamed that one day she would be the slim, trim founder of a renowned company that has helped millions lose weight. But when she devised a method that worked for her—after all others had failed—she simply had to share it with the world.

Throughout her childhood in New York, Jean was a compulsive eater. Unlike many fat children, Jean didn't suffer from her obesity in school. "I was popular because I was a talker and I developed a circle of friends, all overweight," she recalled.

In 1947, at the age of twenty-four, Jean married Martin Nidetch. Of their courtship she has written, "We ate together. We didn't

> "*Everything you do in life helps you—if you know how to file it away and pull it out when you need it.*"

go dancing or bowling or roller-skating. We ate." At the time of her wedding, she wore a size eighteen with the sides let out.

Throughout the 1950s, Jean remained a housewife and mother of two while her husband was an airport-bus driver. They lived in a modest apartment in Queens. She kept busy during the day by joining a variety of organizations. "I became involved in anything that came my way," she recalled. "And whatever organization I got into, I usually ended up heading it."

Despite her busy life, Jean continued to eat compulsively. Not that she didn't try to lose weight. She was a professional dieter who had tried every diet and appetite suppressant pill that she could find. Each time she dieted, she would lose weight, but then she would return to her old eating habits and become heavier than ever.

At the same time, her husband continued to gain weight, too. "We developed a whole act about our size and we were the life of every party," said Jean. "People waited for us to say something funny, and we usually did. After all, if you're fat, you have to make a joke about your weight before somebody else does."

By 1961, Jean was thirty-eight years old, stood five feet, seven inches, and weighed 214 pounds. She hit a low point that year when an acquaintance bumped into her at the supermarket and told Jean, "You look so marvelous. When are you due?" Jean was not pregnant.

In her biography, Jean said the remark "really hurt." She added, "I didn't like the girl then and I don't now, but I've been grateful to her ever since. Most fat people need to be badly hurt before they do something about themselves."

Embarrassed and upset, Jean—who had tried most every eating plan and been to most every diet doctor in the New York area—entered a program at the New York City Department of Health's obesity clinic.

She was given a diet and instructed to follow it with no substitutions, and told she would lose at least two pounds a week until she reached her goal weight of 142 pounds. For ten weeks she followed the diet faithfully—except that each night she locked herself in the bathroom and gorged on cookies.

Unable to confide her weakness to her family or the teacher and members of her dieting class, Jean decided she had to talk to someone. "I found I couldn't do it on a diet alone. I had to be able to talk about my eating problems, to tell other people what I was going through. So I called up a few fat friends and asked them to come to my house to talk. They came."

With her six overweight friends, she discovered that she could freely confess all her dieting sins. They, in turn, shared their failings.

"I needed the girls," said Jean. "I needed to be able to tell them about my difficulties. I've found that all overweight people have this tremendous desire to talk. Maybe we're all 'oral' types—we have to eat or talk."

After the second meeting, she quit the obesity clinic classes because she was able to accomplish more through her own meetings. Her six friends agreed to go on the diet with her. But then an amazing thing happened—the group grew in numbers. "They came every week after that, bringing other fat people with them. It was our little group where we met to tell each other about being fat." Within two months, forty women were meeting at Jean's home.

With their support and encouragement, Jean lost pound after pound. Shortly after her thirty-ninth birthday, she reached her goal of 142 pounds.

Embracers of Opportunity

Having exorcised her own food demons, Jean replaced her compulsion to eat with a desire to help others lose weight. She aided her overweight relatives—including her husband, son, mother, and sister.

Meanwhile, an increasing number of overweight people were meeting in her home. When the size of the groups became too unwieldy, she moved the meetings to the basement of her apartment building. Meanwhile, she was receiving telephone calls from fat people begging for help. So Jean began making house calls and speaking to groups throughout the New York area. She even toted a large weight scale to weigh people. Her exhausting volunteer work brought her satisfaction, but did little to help the family finances.

She finally realized that she held in her hands an enormous business opportunity to help others while making money.

"Every experience has its place in your life," Jean said. "Things that I did years ago are bearing fruit, just like being fat, and all the things I went through as a fat woman help me to help other people now. I know how fat people feel. It never occurred to me at the time that I would ever be telling a huge audience the story of wearing drapes as a costume, that the humiliation of *having* to wear drapes because nothing else would cover me up would one day do some good and be inspirational to others."

In 1963, when she was forty years old, Jean became president of Weight Watchers, a modest company that operated in a loft over a movie theater in Little Neck, New York. Her business was an immediate success. With the help of astute friends, she began to franchise Weight Watchers. Eventually hundreds of thousands of people were gathering each week in classes run by formerly fat people like Jean to talk about losing weight.

"It's people gathering together to talk about their eating habits," Jean said. "What they eat. Why they eat. How they eat. And to be told by the leader or lecturer of the group how to eat properly. It works. Compulsive eating is an emotional problem, and we use an emotional approach to its solution. To me, this is just plain common sense."

In 1973, Weight Watchers celebrated its tenth anniversary at a gala reunion at Madison Square Garden. where thousands of members were entertained by Bob Hope, Pearl Bailey, and other celebrities. "Look, there have been plenty of diets around and plenty of people who have lost weight," Jean told a reporter at the time. "But what makes Weight

Embracers of Opportunity

Watchers different is that, ten years later, we can stage a big reunion and twenty thousand people will show up at Madison Square Garden still keeping their weight off. That is what makes our program succeed."

Since she began Weight Watchers, Jean has appeared on thousands of radio and TV shows and has written several books. In 1995 Weight Watchers International and Weight Watchers Food Co. reported combined sales of $730 million.

"My little private club has become an industry," said Jean. "I never intended it to. It was really just a group for me and my fat friends." But the formerly fat housewife couldn't pass up the opportunity to help others.

Margaret Rudkin

Margaret Rudkin had no great ambition to run her own business. She was content to be a wife and mother. But when opportunity came knocking, she threw open the door and embraced it—and it changed her life.

In 1928, when she was thirty-one years old, Margaret and her husband Albert, a successful stockbroker, bought land in Fairfield, Connecticut, and built a Tudor-style house. They moved their family there the following year, and named the estate Pepperidge Farm, after an old pepperidge (tupelo) tree on the property.

In 1937, the asthma in one of her sons grew worse, so the doctor put him on a

> *"They say life begins at forty. Well, it's certainly true in my case."*

special diet. The doctor suggested to Margaret that she feed her son homemade bread.

"I had never baked bread in my life," Margaret recalled. "I was forty and had no experience. I turned to the reliable *Boston Cookbook* and started following directions. And then, suddenly, I seemed to remember the way my grandmother did it when I was six years old."

Margaret soon discovered that she had an untapped talent for baking. Her family loved her bread. After Margaret gave several loaves to her son's physician, he asked her to make bread for some of his other patients, which she did. They all raved about how good it tasted.

It was then that Margaret saw an opportunity. She thought other people would enjoy eating tasty bread made the old-fashioned way with natural ingredients. So one day in the fall of 1937, she made extra bread and asked her grocer to sell it for her.

The bread sold very quickly. Soon Margaret began selling her bread to other stores and before long was making daily deliveries to several local stores and the exclusive Charles & Co. of New York. When she had trouble keeping up with the orders, she hired several women to help her bake bread in her kitchen. Business kept growing, so she converted the stables and part of the garage on the farm into a bakery.

Margaret made her bread out of slow-aged, unbleached white flour; 93-score sweet creamery butter; fresh whole milk; yeast; water; salt; honey; and cane syrup. No yeast foods or commercial shortenings were ever used. The dough was mixed in small batches, and then cut and kneaded by hand.

After a year, Margaret was baking four thousand loaves a week. To keep up with demand, she moved her bakery into an empty service station in Norwalk, Connecticut. Once she understood her market—consumers who wanted quality baked goods and were willing to pay for them—she began making melba toast and pound cake.

Uncompromising in her standards, Margaret traveled to Minnesota to buy top-grade wheat and had it shipped to local mills where it was ground into flour. Wanting better quality control, she had her company build its own mill based on the principles of the old-time gristmills.

Although she wanted her bread to be a link to the past, Margaret was forced to make some changes. Each loaf was wrapped by machines.

Success after Forty

Because Margaret believed that old-fashioned bread should be cut just before it is eaten, her bread was sold unsliced. But consumer demand eventually forced her to preslice her bread by machine.

Pepperidge Farm did very little advertising because Margaret let her products stand on their own merits and word of mouth.

During the 1950s, Margaret traveled extensively throughout Europe, looking for, in her opinion, the perfect cookies to bring back to the United States. She found them in Belgium. Reaching an agreement with the House of Delacre, a famous Belgian bakery, Margaret obtained the rights to use their recipes and bakery techniques. So, intent on baking these cookies the way they were made in Europe, Margaret imported a 150-foot oven from Belgium. In 1956, she began marketing a new line of the delicate luxury cookies.

Today, the company started by a forty-year-old Connecticut house-wife is a subsidiary of Campbell Soup Co., employing more than five thousand workers and reporting sales in 1995 of $580 million.

— Losers Who Won —

Our great glory is not in never failing,
but in rising every time we fail.

— Confucius

Abraham Lincoln

After the age of forty, Abraham Lincoln felt the sting of rejection time and again from voters and leaders in his own political party. But he refused to believe he was a failure.

The son of a poor frontier farmer, Lincoln worked as an itinerant laborer before moving to New Salem, Illinois, where he clerked in a general store that soon failed.

"Always bear in mind that your own resolution to succeed is more important than any one thing."

Success after Forty

Undeterred, he and a partner teamed up to open their own shop. Lincoln bought a stock of goods on credit, but the business failed within a matter of months, leaving Lincoln with a debt that took years for him to clear. (His conscientious efforts to pay off his debts earned him the nickname "Honest Abe.")

Though he had attended school for a total of less than one year, the self-taught Lincoln was passionately interested in politics and made speeches on subjects to anyone who would listen to him.

In 1832, at the age of twenty-three, Lincoln decided to run for a seat in the Illinois House of Representatives. To help his campaign, he volunteered to fight Indians in the Black Hawk War. He never saw battle and the voters in his district were unimpressed with him. Lincoln finished eighth in a field of thirteen candidates.

Undeterred, he tried again two years later and was elected to the state legislature, where he remained through four terms. Twice, Lincoln was the Whig Party's candidate for speaker, and twice he was defeated. But Lincoln emerged as the floor leader for his party, and he proved to be a skillful and hardworking party organizer. He also went on record opposing slavery because it was "founded on both injustice and bad policy."

Lincoln had recognized that his success in life would depend upon improving his education. He studied grammar as an aid to clear, effective speaking and writing. Encouraged by a successful Springfield lawyer, Lincoln borrowed the leading law textbooks of the era and religiously studied them. He obtained a license to practice law in 1836 when he was twenty-five years old.

Lincoln was so poor that he arrived in Springfield on a borrowed horse and with all his personal property in his saddlebags. With courts in Springfield in session only a few weeks during the year, lawyers had to travel the circuit in order to make a living. Every year, in spring and fall, Lincoln followed the judge from county to county.

In 1843, when he was thirty-four, Lincoln set his sights on election to the U.S. House of Representatives. His ambition was twice thwarted by his failure to obtain the nomination. "I feel just like the boy who stubbed his toe—too damned badly hurt to laugh and too damned proud to cry," Lincoln said ruefully. But he finally succeeded and took his seat in 1847 at the age of thirty-eight.

Success after Forty

His term in Congress was a disappointment to him and to his constituents. He opposed the Mexican War, then in progress, although he voted for supplies for troops in the field. He backed the official Whig position, but it did not endear him to the people of his district, most of whom were ardently for the war. Because of his antiwar stand, he knew he couldn't get reelected and didn't bother to run.

In 1848, he campaigned vigorously for the Whig ticket and Zachary Taylor's successful bid for the presidency. But Lincoln was denied the political plum that he wanted—appointment as commissioner of the General Land Office.

It was one of many political setbacks to come for the middle-aged Lincoln. Bitterly disappointed, the forty-year-old former congressman retired from politics and returned to Illinois to build up his law practice.

Over the next five years, he virtually ignored the political limelight and concentrated on being one of the area's best lawyers. He represented major corporations and defended ordinary citizens. Although he sharpened his legal skills, Lincoln couldn't get politics out of his blood. He loved it too much.

Losers Who Won

"It was in the world of politics that he lived," said his former law partner and later biographer William Herndon. "Politics were his life, newspapers were his food."

In 1854, the married forty-five-year-old attorney and father of three boys returned to politics because he felt there was a purpose bigger than himself; he had a mission to complete. Lincoln became outraged after Senator Stephen A. Douglas (D-Ill) pushed his controversial Kansas-Nebraska Act through Congress. In effect, this legislation allowed inhabitants of the newly-opened territories to decide whether or not they wanted slavery. Congress previously had agreed to close slavery to this large area.

Lincoln actively campaigned for Richard Yates, the local Whig candidate who, as a member of Congress, had voted against the Kansas-Nebraska Act. Lincoln's speeches suddenly took on new depth and fervor. He began receiving invitations to speak in cities beyond his own congressional district.

Lincoln's stature grew. Early in 1855, Lincoln narrowly missed being chosen for the U.S. Senate when the Illinois legislature met to elect a successor to Senator James Shield. Lincoln remained loyal to his old party until the Whigs collapsed. In 1856, he joined the new Republican Party and campaigned for its presidential candidate, John Frémont, who eventually lost to James Buchanan.

In 1858, Lincoln, then forty-nine, was the Republican's choice to oppose Douglas's reelection bid to the Senate. Lincoln challenged his opponent to a series of debates to be held in the seven congressional districts of the state in which the two candidates had not yet spoken. Reluctantly, Douglas accepted.

Lincoln opened his campaign with the famous declaration "A house divided against itself cannot stand. I believe this government cannot endure permanently half slave and half free."

In early August, both candidates embarked on speaking tours that lasted until November. The goal of each was the election of his own party members to the state legislature, which would choose the U.S. senator in joint session. The contest called for constant travel by horse and buggy, steamboats, and the primitive railroads of the time. The men had to speak in all kinds of weather, taxing them to the limit of their endurance.

Losers Who Won

Lincoln gave it everything he had. But once again, he lost. Yet he had gained politically in other ways. The campaign had given Lincoln a national reputation that soon led to speaking engagements outside of Illinois.

In 1860, the Republicans held their convention to choose a presidential candidate. Although Senator William Seward of New York and Ohio governor Salmon Chase were the most popular, the delegates picked Lincoln on the third ballot.

Five months later, Lincoln, running on an antislavery platform, was elected president of the United States, beating out three other candidates, including his arch rival Stephen Douglas.

But then the Civil War erupted. The man who had experienced so many failures in politics showed his greatness as president by holding the country together in its darkest hours. His passion for what he believed was right can still be felt today in his words in the Gettysburg and Inaugural Addresses and the Emancipation Proclamation.

Harry Truman

Harry Truman knew failure firsthand in business and in politics. But he never dwelled on it. Instead, he learned from his failures and kept marching forward, always doing the best he could.

Growing up in Independence, Missouri, Truman obtained an appointment to West Point but was rejected because of his poor eyesight. Not sure what he wanted to do with his life, he worked in a drugstore and on a railroad construction crew before becoming a bank employee in Kansas City.

At the age of twenty-two, Truman, at the request of his father who was suffering financial difficulties, returned to his roots and became a farmer for the next twelve years. Although he didn't really want to be a farmer, he gave it his all.

> "When I failed, I always went ahead and did the best I could without taking time out to worry about how it would have been if it had worked out a better way."

oy could plow the straightest row of corn in the county," his

boasted. "He could sow wheat so there would not be a bare
spot in the whole field. He was a farmer and could do anything there was
to do just a little better than anyone else."

The farm meant much loneliness, but Truman turned it to his advantage. It offered him the opportunity to read and study the philosophy of history's great leaders. He considered principles of right and wrong and how honesty and integrity counted. He understood—when he got into politics—that compromise meant arriving at a mutually agreeable position without giving up one's principles.

Truman had developed a love for politics from his father. In his first political appointment, Truman succeeded his father as road overseer for the southern part of the township. This required Truman to spend his spare time collecting taxes, repairing culverts and bridges, and dragging dirty roads after the rain with an eight-mule grader, for a salary of five dollars a day. But he eventually resigned his post because of a disagreement with his superiors over his harping for the need for more improvements.

A few days after the United States entered World War I, the thirty-three-year-old farmer, who was a member of the National Guard, was sworn in as a first lieutenant in the army. He passed the physical exam by arranging to have the examining sergeant prompt him on the eye chart.

Shipped overseas, Truman was given command of an artillery battery in France that had worn out five previous captains. After an inauspicious beginning during which the assembled battery greeted the quiet, bespectacled farmer with a Bronx cheer, he brought the men under control through a careful combination of firmness and friendliness. "Captain Harry," as they fondly called him, then led them through several fierce battles without losing a man.

In 1919, six weeks after his return at the end of the war, the thirty-five-year-old Truman married Bess Wallace—the only girl he ever went with. Although happy on the home front, Truman was about to face several setbacks in his career.

He went into partnership with a friend in a Kansas City haberdashery. "The store made out well for a while," Truman recalled. "But its earnings were plowed back into inventory; its contracts were at boom levels; and when business sagged, the haberdashery was squeezed to pieces in the recession of 1921." Truman lost his entire savings of $15,000, plus another $20,000. Against the advice of friends, Truman refused to file for bankruptcy, saving for fifteen years to pay off his debts.

Meanwhile, Tom Pendergast, boss of the local Democratic machine, nominated Truman as a candidate for the local county commission. Truman won and took office in 1923 when he was thirty-nine years old. Figuring that "knowing a little law wouldn't hurt," Truman enrolled for evening courses at the Kansas City School of Law, but he never graduated.

At the age of forty-one, Truman lost his political seat when his constituents voted him out of office, partly because of his vocal opposition to the Ku Klux Klan. Truman dusted himself off and went into a different line of work. He helped organize the Kansas City Automobile Club, and within less than two years he built up the membership to more than three thousand.

Truman tried again to get back into politics, but failed to win the party's nomination to the $25,000-a-year county collectorship. Refusing to give up, he tried again. This time, he was elected to a county position in which he had charge of the spending of sixty million dollars for highways and public buildings in Jackson County at a salary of $6,300 a year. "We built more miles of paved roads in Jackson County than any other county in the nation, with two exceptions," he boasted. Truman even had a surplus which, he confessed, he spent on a statue of Andrew Jackson.

Truman leaned over backward to be honest. To avoid the appearance of favoritism, he refused to pay his mother for the eleven acres taken from her farm for a county boulevard, even though she was entitled to eleven thousand dollars in compensation.

After eight years of overseeing the county's road-building, Truman faced political disappointment. He asked Pendergast to nominate him for a more lucrative position as the county tax collector, but Pendergast turned him down. Then he asked for the nomination to represent a new congressional district. Once again, the Democratic machine said no.

By now, he was fifty years old. But Truman's disappointment soon turned to happiness. His name had grown in stature and his honesty was above reproach—traits not lost on the Democratic state chairman, who asked Truman to run for the U.S. Senate. Truman did, and in 1936 he was overwhelmingly elected.

Success after Forty

Despite the exposure of corruption in the Pendergast organization, Truman was reelected in 1940, though narrowly. He won partially on the strength of his personal integrity and loyalty to President Roosevelt's New Deal. During his second Senate term, his chairing of an investigation of war profiteering, military expenditures, and defense production brought him national recognition.

Truman never aspired to higher office. He once said, "Three things can ruin a man—money, power, and women. I never had any money, I never wanted power, and the only woman in my life is up at the house right now."

Following an intraparty fight in 1944, the Democratic Party chose Truman to replace Henry A. Wallace as Roosevelt's running mate. After Roosevelt was reelected for the fourth time, Truman served as vice president for only eighty-three days. To the shock of the nation, the president died unexpectedly in 1945. Suddenly, the farmer and failed haberdashery owner was catapulted into the highest office in the country.

Never one to shirk responsibility, Truman authorized the first uses of the atomic bomb, bringing World War II to a rapid end. Under his leadership, NATO and the Marshall Plan were created and the Berlin Airlift was launched. When Communist North Korea invaded South Korea, he won United Nations approval to send in forces. Truman was credited for raising the minimum wage and increasing Social Security and aid-for-housing laws.

"I studied the lives of great men and famous women, and I found that the men and women who got to the top were those who did the jobs they had in hand, with everything they had of energy and enthusiasm and hard work," he said.

"When you give everything that is in you to do the job you have before you, that's all you can ask of yourself—and that's what I have tried to do."

John Glenn

John Glenn had soared to success as a Marine fighter pilot and as an astronaut. But once he entered the political arena, he was shot down. Becoming a U.S. senator mattered most to him. And despite his failures, he kept going when most people suggested he quit—and he found a way to accomplish his goal.

In 1959, at the age of thirty-eight, John Glenn—a Marine fighter pilot and test pilot for sixteen years—was chosen as one of the original seven astronauts by NASA. Although he was the oldest of the magnificent seven, he was determined to show up the younger ones. Under a rigorous personal schedule, Glenn ran two miles every day and dieted to bring his

> *"You can't let failure get you down or it will keep you down."*

weight down from 195 to 168 pounds. He studied books, charts, and maps in the evening. To concentrate on his work, he lived in bachelor quarters during the week and visited his family in Virginia only on weekends.

Two years later, the forty-year-old Glenn was named as the astronaut who would make the first U.S. orbital spaceflight. The honor proved to be a test of his patience. The mission was postponed an incredible ten times over two months because of technical difficulties or weather conditions. Once, he lay in his capsule for more than five hours, waiting for a liftoff that didn't happen.

During the delays between each scrubbed mission, Glenn filled his time by studying, practicing in the simulation trainers, and improving his ability to hand-control the capsule. He urged his fellow Americans to stay calm. "This mission has been in preparation for a long time," he said. "I'm so happy to have been chosen to be the pilot for this mission that I'm not about to get panicky over these delays. I learned early in the flight-test business that you have to control your emotions. You don't let these things throw you or affect your ability to perform the mission."

Finally, at 9:47 A.M. on February 20, 1962, Glenn was boosted aloft in his capsule *Friendship 7* to begin his historic flight. But at the end of the first orbit, the astronaut faced a major problem—the automatic control mechanism for the jets that stabilized the craft failed. Glenn coolly took over manual control of the capsule and finished the planned three-orbit flight of 81,000 miles.

"I was fully aware of the danger," he later told reporters. "And certainly there was apprehension. No matter what preparation you make, there comes the moment of truth. You're playing with big stakes—your life. But the important thing to me wasn't fear, but what you can do to control it.

"A lot of people ask why a man is willing to risk hat, tail, and gas mask on something like this spaceflight. I've got a theory about this. People are afraid of the future, of the unknown. If a man faces up to it and takes the dare of the future, he can have some control over his destiny. That's an exciting idea to me, better than waiting with everybody else to see what's going to happen."

Upon his safe return, Glenn became the nation's greatest peacetime hero. Trying to describe the national reaction to the event, author Thomas

Wolfe noted that "tears ran like a river all over America. . . . That was what the sight of John Glenn did to Americans at that time. It primed them for the tears."

But Glenn's life took a dramatic shift the following year. Profoundly affected by the assassination of President John F. Kennedy on November 22, 1963, Glenn resigned from the space program two months later to pursue a new career in politics at the age of forty-two. "I decided to reassess my views as to my responsibilities and where we were going in this country," he recalled. "I decided I would run for the Senate. I didn't want to do it as an ego trip. The challenge is to make a better place for the people still to come."

To Glenn, the Senate was a logical extension of his previous public service because "that's where there's clout." He added, "Why should I negotiate at the county commissioner level?"

What he lacked in political experience he felt he had made up in serving his country: "I've looked at my service in the Marine Corps and the post–World War II days as being public service. I was proud of service to my country in World War II, and stayed in the Marine Corps through the

Losers Who Won

Korean War to test pilot work and the space program. And I guess at the age I was at [forty-two], when I came out of the space program . . . I felt if there were other areas I could serve my country in, well, I couldn't think of any other use to which I could put my life [except as a senator]. I've had enough attention to last me several lifetimes. So I get a great satisfaction being able to work on some of the things that not only will help solve some of the problems we have here in this country, but perhaps more important, to help outline the opportunities—things toward which we could go in the future."

Brimming with enthusiasm, Glenn entered the Ohio Democratic primary in 1964 only to be waylaid by misfortune. He fell in the bathroom and suffered an injury to his inner ear. It affected his balance so badly that he was forced to withdraw from the race after only two months on the campaign trail.

Glenn then turned his attention to several successful business enterprises before again running for the Senate in 1970. He believed that the public automatically would nominate him in the primary because they had made him a folk hero. "Glenn didn't do much but say, 'I'm John

Success after Forty

Glenn—here I am, vote for me,'" wrote one reporter.

But one of Glenn's major attributes—his astronaut hero image—was also a liability. Recalled Glenn, "I had studied the issues and prepared what I thought were good positions, but I'd walk into a meeting and the first question I'd hear would be 'Do astronauts really drink Tang?'"

Glenn campaigned largely on his name recognition and was stunned when he lost the primary by thirteen thousand votes. His opponent, Howard Metzenbaum, beat him because the veteran had the support of the Democratic Party, better organization, more money, and experience. Recalled Glenn, "Two wars, cross-country speed record, orbital flight, and then to be rejected by my home state. It wasn't very pleasant.

"We got a late start, we didn't get the right people, and we had no money." In short, he was a poor campaigner who ran a poor campaign.

Glenn vowed to learn from his mistakes. He would not back away from his goal. He felt the Senate was where he needed to be and he was going to work extra-hard to make sure he got there. He pledged to himself that he wouldn't make the same mistakes again—and that he would win.

"I decided to stay right in and work with the party and make as many contacts as we could within the state and be as active in the party as I could," he said. "So I did during that time period after 1970. I don't think anyone in the whole state, with the possible exception of the governor, spoke at more Jefferson-Jackson Day dinners or fund-raising dinners for different candidates or worked more closely with county, local, and state Democratic officials than I did. When we came into the 1974 campaign, we could organize it on a completely different basis—a much broader area of contact and support."

Unfortunately, Glenn was faced with trying to beat Metzenbaum again. Although Metzenbaum had lost the 1970 general election, he had been appointed to a vacancy in the Senate. Ohio governor John Gilligan and other party leaders wanted him to run for the Senate again. Hoping to avoid an intraparty battle, the Democratic powerbrokers offered to support Glenn for lieutenant governor instead of for senator. If Glenn went along, they said, they would back him for the Senate in 1976 or for governor in 1978.

Their proposal angered Glenn. "I didn't think what they were doing was right," Glenn said. "I felt I had earned my opportunity by my life in public service to run for the Senate. . . . I did not want to be told what to do. I saw myself as fulfilling a better role than lieutenant governor. . . . This was my time. If I didn't run for senator, I was going to do something else in public service—maybe go with a foundation. . . . Besides, I don't like deals."

Glenn turned down the package and declared his candidacy. It put him in a familiar position—running against his party's incumbent senator (as in 1964) and running against his party's organization (as in 1970). This time, however, his prospects were brighter. His politicking had put him in a better position to appeal to the party's rank and file.

Richard F. Fenno Jr., author of *The Presidential Odyssey of John Glenn,* wrote: "His confrontation with the governor and the party hierarchy was an important learning experience for Glenn. It did as much as any single event in his political career to shape his political persona. It solidified his public service view of politics. It helped him carve out a degree of political independence. It uncovered his Marine combativeness that could be effective politically as well as militarily. It established him as a resourceful political counterpuncher. It brought him a new level of respect as a political figure."

Billing himself as "someone your children can look up to," Glenn called for a return to integrity in government and for "the restoration of confidence" in public officials.

Glenn ran a vigorous campaign against Metzenbaum and whipped the party-supported incumbent in the 1974 primary. Glenn then trounced the Republican candidate by a two-to-one margin. At the age of fifty-three, John Glenn had reached his goal. At the time he was one of only four senators who were older than fifty when elected and who had never held elective office.

Glenn came to the Senate as an amateur, a person with everything to learn about politics. He had learned—through defeat—how to campaign for the Senate. He was a "mature amateur" in politics, starting late in life and carrying with him no political experience. He had to learn a new profession while still under the influence of his old profession. He had to blend the indelible lessons of his earlier career with the changing requirements of his later career.

As a freshman senator, Glenn became a leading spokesman for a national energy policy and a strong advocate of campaign financing reform. He has since been reelected to the Senate three times.

While recalling his journey to the Senate, Glenn drew on his Marine fighter pilot background: "I never pulled out high over targets. I was the one who went in low and got them—and as a result I was known as Old Magnet Tail."

— FOLLOWERS OF THE HEART —

Every calling is great when greatly pursued.

— Oliver Wendell Holmes Jr.

Maggie Kuhn

Maggie Kuhn burst onto the national scene when she was sixty-five because she acted on her strong belief that age discrimination is as fundamental and poisonous a force as racism or sexism. She was intent on wiping out ageism.

Kuhn had devoted much of her life to fighting for the rights of others. Social

> *"You can start a completely new career after the age of sixty and go on if necessary until you're eighty."*

consciousness became a strong force in her life from the very beginning. Shortly before Maggie was born in 1905, her mother moved from Memphis to Buffalo so that Maggie wouldn't be born in the South, where segregation was practiced at the time.

After receiving a college degree in English, Kuhn worked for eleven years at a variety of jobs organizing young, unemployed women for the YWCA in Cleveland and Philadelphia. "So many of our members at the YWCA were women working for rotten-paying clerical or commercial jobs," she recalled. "They were working six days a week for ten dollars. In the depression, of course, it got worse. My work with these women, as they started to organize and unionize, cemented my radicalism."

Eventually, Kuhn began a twenty-five-year professional career with the United Presbyterian Church in New York, where she served as associate secretary in the office of church and society and as coordinator of programming in the division of church and race. She also helped edit and write a church magazine.

In 1969, at the age of sixty-four, Kuhn was working as a program executive for the church's Council on Church and Race. But she was involved in a number of social action projects, including work on a subcommittee on the problems of the old. "My interest in these issues was not personal," she recalled. "The facts appealed to me as an activist. Many of us in the churches were concerned about the soaring poverty among the elderly and the staggering growth of the country's aged population."

By 1969 there were twenty million people sixty-five years or older, and the number was growing at a rate of nine-hundred a day. Nearly one-fourth of the aged population was living below the poverty line. Medical costs were skyrocketing. Private pensions were unreliable and social services for the old were inadequate.

"Dissatisfaction among the nation's old had been growing for two decades," Kuhn said. "When the Senate Subcommittee on the Problems of the Aged and Aging held hearings around the country in 1959, older Americans lined up to testify about the trials of their lives. They spoke of loneliness, destitution, and alienation.

"The church's interest in the old was largely confined to administering to the sick and dying and running retirement homes for the well-to-do Presbyterians. Many church officials, failing to see that the old needed vastly more than the church was giving them, did not detect the rebellion brewing."

Back then, programs for the elderly were almost exclusively recreational—activities such as bingo and arts and crafts. "There seemed to be an apathy and malaise among the people in these programs that I could not attribute to old age itself," Kuhn recalled. "The women all wore polyester pantsuits with the same cut. There was a heart-wrenching monotony to their days. Was this what old age was meant to be?

"Truthfully, in those years, I didn't think of myself as about to enter the ranks of the nation's old either. I was just me—neither young, old, nor middle-aged. All of that changed when I was sixty-four."

About seven months before her sixty-fifth birthday, Kuhn faced a major shock. She was told to retire. "I had never given retirement much thought. I had hoped the Church would ask me to stay on in my job on a year-to-year basis. As I felt energetic enough to go on for many years, the idea of retiring struck me as ludicrous and depressing. My work was my whole life. I couldn't envision myself with no serious purpose in life and cut off from the wide circle of friends at work. I was worried I'd end up becoming completely immersed in the care of my aging brother."

Kuhn was allowed to finish out the year to give her time to get her affairs in order and to prepare for her new life. "In the first month after I was ordered to retire, I felt dazed and suspended. I was hurt and then, as time passed, outraged. I came to a great kinship with my peers and to believe that something was fundamentally wrong with a system that had no use for people like us."

Instead of sinking into despair and finishing out her life in misery, Kuhn decided to fight back, using all the experience she had garnered over the years to her advantage. She had a purpose and a goal. And she was determined to succeed in making big changes for the elderly and society.

The first thing she did was phone friends who were also nearing or at retirement age. All were veteran activists who had energy to spare. She gathered them together for a meeting.

"We didn't feel old," Kuhn recalled. "In fact, we felt more radical and full of new ideas, more opinionated and less constrained by convention than we were when we graduated from college. We knew our lives had reached a sort of climax, not an ending. Yet we felt disturbed that we had few role models. Many of our mothers and grandmothers had been active up to the very end of their lives, but they were at home. We wanted to continue to be involved in social action bearing on the important issues of the day."

The small group then held a larger gathering, inviting people who were concerned about older persons and the issues of the 1970s. More than one hundred people attended and discussed ways retirees could be involved in new and significant ways in business and society. The meeting led to the formation of the Consultation of Older Persons, a group of retired men and women who proposed new programs for social action. They shared a sense of freedom to act upon their beliefs without feeling bound by the constrictions of their former roles in corporate bureaucracy.

The five-foot, three-inch, 105-pound, gray-haired dynamo began speaking to whoever would listen. She knew that if she kept working at her cause, she would get the one big break that would thrust her organization into the national spotlight. It came sooner than she thought.

Followers of the Heart

One day Kuhn shared a cab with a producer of a TV talk show. He suggested she change the name of the Consultation of Older Persons. "You know, that name doesn't sound like what you have in mind," he said. "I think you should call it the Gray Panthers."

Kuhn agreed—and soon so did the members of the group, which adopted the new name. "Gray is a symbolic color," she said. "Everyone gets old, and if you put all the colors of the rainbow together, you get gray."

As word of the Gray Panthers spread, Kuhn became in great demand for interviews in dozens of newspapers, magazines, and on talks shows. "All of a sudden, I had none of the former constraints," she recalled. "I was free to speak my mind—and believe me, I did."

Letters by the thousands poured in from people of all ages, mostly elderly, who identified with Kuhn's cause.

Her little coalition of old as well as young members set about forming a national grass-roots organization in 1973. Two years later, when Kuhn was seventy, the Gray Panthers held its first national convention. The final body of resolutions reflected the organization's far-reaching and eclectic goals—reduction of military spending, a new health system, an end to compulsory retirement and age discrimination in employment, and new housing options for young and old.

The Gray Panthers have since staged demonstrations, written position papers, lobbied for new laws, and monitored operations of the courts, banks, insurance companies, and the media. Today the Gray Panthers have tens of thousands of members in fifty-eight chapters in the United States and five other countries.

Reflecting on her successes, Kuhn once said, "Too many men and women are thrown on the scrap heap when they are sixty. It's nonsense to think a person is too old at sixty. You can start a completely new career and go on if necessary until you're eighty. It's too easy to sit back and vegetate in retirement."

In 1980, at the age of seventy-five, Kuhn founded the National Shared Housing Resource Center, where young and old live together for the benefit of both. "I passionately believe that there must be more of these sorts of living arrangements," she said. "The old have been brainwashed to believe that it is safer and nicer to be with their peers in retirement communities or age-segregated organizations. Indeed, for some that may be the answer, but for increasing numbers, I believe it is not. Many old people find such arrangements confining and bleak. They want to be around young people. And young people want to be with them."

Kuhn practiced what she preached. She shared her stone town house with an assortment of young people. Just before her death in 1995 at the age of ninety, she finished an article for the Gray Panther newsletter, It ended with the words: "We are Age and Youth in Action."

Mother Jones

Perhaps no American used age to her advantage more than Mother Jones. She fashioned her advancing age into a shield against thugs, authorities, and employers intent on thwarting her causes. She participated in many of the great turn-of-the-century strikes against railroad barons, meat packers, steel magnates, textile oligarches, and coal mine owners.

Irish-born Mary Harris grew up in Toronto to become a teacher and then a dressmaker. In 1861, at the age of thirty-one, she moved to Memphis where she met and married George Jones, an iron molder. The couple had four children over the next six years. Although they didn't have much, Mary felt content and

> "*Age means nothing when you do what's right in your heart.*"

enjoyed her life with her loving family. But then tragedy struck. In the summer of 1867, a yellow-fever epidemic swept through Memphis. In one horrific week, Mary lost her husband and all her children. "I sat alone through nights of grief," she wrote in her autobiography. "No one came. No one could. Other homes were stricken, just as mine." Mary Jones was left a widow at the age of thirty-seven.

The devastated widow moved to Chicago and resumed her work as a dressmaker. Incredibly, tragedy plagued her life again, when the Chicago fire of 1871 burned down her home and destroyed all her possessions.

Mary had lost virtually everything she held dear. But at least she had her life, albeit a sad one. Mary stood at the crossroads. She was a forty-one-year-old, lonely, penniless widow with no future and a heartwrenching past. She could have given up. Instead, she reached inside her soul and discovered an inner strength to help others.

She found her purpose in life after taking shelter with hundreds of other fire victims in a church basement. She wandered into the meetings being held nearby by the Knights of Labor, the industrial union that had been founded as a secret society among Philadelphia garment workers in

Followers of the Heart

1869. She responded enthusiastically to the Knights' rhetoric and decided that instead of wallowing in self-pity over her personal plight, she would devote her life to the labor movement.

Back then labor had no rights. Owners dictated wages, hours of work, and working conditions. Child labor was a mainstay of industry. Little girls, some as young as seven, made up a large percentage of the textile workforce. In the anthracite coalfields, boys spent their childhood hunched over coal chutes, picking slate from the cascading coal.

Mary Jones burned with a fierce determination as she worked ceaselessly on behalf of the exploited class. She served a long apprenticeship, sometimes as an official representative of the Knights and other times as a missionary to the working poor.

By 1877, when she was forty-seven, the small but sturdy activist was widely known as "Mother Jones" because of her matronly manner. She always wore a bonnet and dressed like a demure spinster, yet her heart beat like a raging lioness. She began receiving national attention that year when she went to Pittsburgh in the heat of the national railroad strike to add her voice to the uproar against the use of federal troops in a labor dispute.

Success after Forty

After the decline of the Knights in the late 1880s, Mother Jones turned her attention to the textile and coal industries. She studied the conditions of child labor in the South firsthand, working in a mill in Cottondale, Alabama, and in a rope factory in Tuscaloosa. There, she saw the plight of the 30 percent of southern mill workers who were under the age of sixteen, yet worked ten to twelve hours a day in the dust-choked air.

A few years later, in the summer of 1903, she led a small army of children, many of them maimed from mill accidents. Her "Children's Crusade" marched from the textile mills of Kensington, Pennsylvania, to the summer home of President Theodore Roosevelt on Long Island to appeal for passage of a federal child labor law. He refused to see them, but her well-publicized march helped develop popular support for national child labor laws.

Mother Jones's most sustained and productive work, however, was among the miners. Drawn to her first coal strike in Norton, Virginia, in 1891 when she was sixty-one, she developed many of the tactics for which she later became noted. Arrested and refused access to meeting halls, she gathered miners around her in the roadways, rallying them to defy authority by her own audacity.

Followers of the Heart

Exploiting her grandmotherly demeanor, Mother Jones wore a bonnet and long, demure dresses flecked with lace. She took advantage of the protective sexism and ageism of her opponents for her own purposes. Often defying guards to shoot her, she escaped almost certain death through her sheer boldness and belief that no one would dare gun down a little old lady. Nevertheless, she was often spat on, kicked, clubbed, and jailed.

Industry attacked her, denouncing her as "a vulgar heartless creature who inflames the ignorant workers to bite the hand that feeds them." Her tactics dismayed even union officials because of the frequent violent confrontations she seemed to provoke. However, those same officials also were impressed with the results she often achieved.

Acknowledging her militantism, Jones explained, "I'm not a humanitarian. I'm a hell-raiser. My philosophy is pray for the dead and fight like hell for the living."

In 1900, the seventy-year-old activist helped lead a successful nine-month strike of miners in eastern Pennsylvania. She organized the miners' wives into a women's brigade that marched on the mines, beating on pots and pans and swinging brooms at the mules that hauled the coal cars to the surface of the mines.

In Colorado, Mother Jones investigated conditions of miners by disguising herself as a peddler. In 1903, she recommended a strike. The walkout led to a quick settlement to the satisfaction of the miners in the northern area. When she tried to lead a strike in southern Colorado, authorities escorted her out of the state. She sneaked back in, only to be quarantined for alleged exposure to smallpox.

The tireless activist refused to quit. She headed a march of two thousand labor delegates to the state capital to protest the use of troops in the dispute. She was arrested and held in a Sisters of Charity hospital for nine weeks.

As soon as she was released, she returned to the strike zone. Colorado authorities then confined her in the cellar of a courthouse for nearly a month. While incarcerated, Mother Jones fought off the sewer rats by pelting them with discarded beer bottles.

Mother Jones participated in five major strikes in West Virginia over a forty-year period in her struggle to unionize the coal fields. The average annual wage there was the nation's lowest for the coal industry. The area was difficult to organize because the miners and their families usually lived in isolated company towns and were totally dependent on their employers.

The 1912–13 strike of bituminous coal workers turned into one of the worst in West Virginia's history. During the fourteen-month mine war, in which fifty persons were killed, she exhorted workers to protect themselves—even if, she said, they had to buy "every gun in Charleston."

Mother Jones tried to seek a meeting with the governor, but a rumor spread that she was leading a force of 3,500 men to assassinate him and dynamite the capitol. Under martial law, armed forces seized Mother Jones, tried her before a military court, and sentenced her to twenty years in prison on a charge of conspiracy to commit murder. Fortunately, a state commission overturned the trumped-up charge. The elderly activist continued her fight. Within six years, about half the state's mines had been organized.

In her last major strike, she helped organize the post-World War I steel walkout led by William Foster. In that dispute, she was jailed again—a few months prior to her ninetieth birthday.

Success after Forty

Mother Jones died in 1930 at the age of one hundred. She was buried in a miners' cemetery in Mount Olive, Illinois, where an imposing monument was erected in her memory. The grand old warhorse had fought countless battles and lost many. But she left a legacy that became the foundation of the American labor movement—a foundation she didn't start building until after the age of forty.

Mother Teresa

Mother Teresa has always followed her heart. It led her from a happy home to a rewarding teaching career to the streets of despair in Calcutta.

Born in 1910 in what was then Yugoslavia, Agnes Gonxha Bojaxhiu (her original name) grew up in a loving Catholic home to working-class parents. "At the age of twelve, I first knew I had a vocation to help the poor," she recalled. "I wanted to be a missionary." But she loved her family so much and had such an exceptionally happy home life that she didn't want to leave it.

When Agnes was fifteen, she was deeply moved after reading of the con-

> "*P*rofound joy of the heart is like a magnet that indicates the path of life. One has to follow it, even though one enters into a way full of difficulties."

ditions in India from Yugoslav Jesuit missionaries who served there. At eighteen, she left home to join the Sisters of Loreto, a community of Irish nuns with a mission in the Archdiocese of Calcutta. After training at Loreto institutions in Dublin, Ireland, and Darjeeling, India, she took her first vows as a nun in 1928 and her final vows nine years later when she was twenty-seven.

She taught and served as principal at St. Mary's High School in Calcutta, which was mostly for middle-class children. She loved teaching. But eventually Mother Teresa was struck by the suffering she glimpsed outside the cloistered walls in the teeming slums of Calcutta: the home-less street urchins, the ostracized lepers, the destitute ill, many lying in streets and alleys, the prey of rats and ants.

"Once I asked my confessor for advice about my vocation," she said. "I asked, 'How can I know if God is calling me and for what he is calling me?' He answered, 'You will know by your happiness. If you are happy with the idea that God calls you to serve him and your neighbor, this will be the proof of your vocation.'"

In 1946, at the age of thirty-six, she received a "call within a call—like a second vocation," as she described it. "The message was clear. I was to leave the convent and help the poor while living among them." Two years later, the Vatican granted her permission to leave Loreto and pursue her new calling under the jurisdiction of the Archbishop of Calcutta. But first she had to receive medical training.

"To leave Loreto was my greatest sacrifice," she said, "the most difficult thing I have ever done. It was much more difficult than to leave my family and country to enter religious life. Loreto meant everything to me. In Loreto I received my spiritual training. I had become religious there. I liked the work, teaching the girls.

"Soon after leaving Loreto, I was on the street, with no shelter, no company, no helper, no money, no employment, no promise, no guarantee, no security. Then I prayed, 'My God, you, only you. I trust in your call, your inspiration. You will not let me down.'"

Mother Teresa walked the Calcutta slums and gathered children who had been cut off from education. She brought them into her first school, which was held out in the open air because she had nowhere else to teach them. Soon, donors responded with money and provided her with facilities. Then volunteers—many of them former students of hers—came to dedicate their lives to serving the poor with her.

In 1950, at the age of forty, Mother Teresa founded her congregation with an initial membership of only twelve. Word of their loving, dedicated work in Calcutta spread around the globe. Fifteen years after the Missionaries of Charity became an official religious community, the Vatican recognized it as a pontifical congregation directly under the jurisdiction of Rome.

The community now has about three thousand sisters and brothers on five continents, although most of the missionaries work in India. Aiding abandoned and poor children and sick and dying adults, the missionaries have taken in tens of thousands of the needy. The congregation has sheltered an untold number of orphans and unwanted children; taught and treated thousands more in its schools and clinics. The missionaries continue to pick up the dying left in gutters and bring them to the shelter, where they are comforted as they face death with dignity.

In accordance with the constitution and rules created by Mother Teresa, the members of the congregation take the traditional vows of poverty, chastity, and obedience. But the vow of poverty is stricter than in other congregations because, as Mother Teresa explained, "To be able to love the poor and know the poor, we must be poor ourselves." In addition to the three traditional vows, the Missionaries of Charity take a unique fourth vow, a promise to give "whole-hearted free service to the poorest of the poor." The vow means that they can't work for the rich or accept any money for what they do.

In 1979, sixty-nine-year-old Mother Teresa achieved worldwide acclaim when she was awarded the Nobel Peace Prize for her devotion to serving the poor. Like so many other awards that she has received, she immediately put the money into helping the poor.

Said the *London Observer:* "Mother Teresa's most astonishing and bewildering characteristic is her lack of any sense of indignation. Mother Teresa reminds one sharply that in the teaching of Christ there is no rage and indignation, no burning desire to change the horrifying injustices of a society that allows such poverty; like it or not, there is only the injunction to love and turn the other cheek."

Mother Teresa has a simple explanation: "I am called to help the individual, to love each poor person, not to deal with institutions."

The tiny, stooped bundle of energy continues her work, traveling the world over, following her heart and her faith. "The miracle is not that we do this work, but that we are happy to do it," she said. "God has not called me to be successful. He called me to be faithful."